Maine Trivia

Also from Islandport Press

Forever Yours, Bar Harbor
Earl Brechlin

Take It Easy
John Duncan

Wild! Weird! Wonderful! Maine.
Earl Brechlin

Speakin' Maine
Dean L. Lunt

Headin' for the Rhubarb
Rebecca Rule

This Day in Maine
Joseph Owen

Downeast Genius
Earl Smith

Making Tracks
Matt Weber

Evergreens
John Holyoke

Maine Trivia

Dean Lunt and John McDonald

ISLANDPORT PRESS

ISLANDPORT PRESS

Islandport Press, Inc.
P.O. Box 10
Yarmouth, Maine 04096
www.islandportpress.com
info@islandportpress.com

ISBN: 978-1-952143-14-4
Library of Congress Control Number: 2021932247

Printed in the United States of America

Dean L. Lunt | Editor-in-Chief, Publisher
Emily E. Boyer | Book Cover Design
Emily A. Lunt | Book Design

To Ann

———

To Vivian

Table of Contents

Maine   1

History   15

Nature & Wildlife   45

Sports   65

Arts & Literature   79

Maine Places   103

Final Round   123

Extra Credit   135

Acknowledgments   149

About the Authors   151

Maine

Where does Maine rank among the fifty states in terms of population?

Forty-second.

According to the 2020 census, Maine's population was 1.36 million. The population increased about 3% compared to 2010.

In what census year did the population of Maine first surpass 500,000?

1840.

Twenty years after statehood, the state checked in with a population of 501,793 people. The population in 1840 increased about 26% when compared to 1830. The population would not cross the one million mark until 1980.

How many miles of coastline does Maine have?

An estimated 225 miles as a crow flies.

However, it's 3,478 miles if you walk the entire length of Maine's picturesque coast along the high-water mark. Maine has the third longest coastline of the 48 continental states, trailing only Louisiana and Florida.

True or False: Maine boasts more than 5,000 lakes and ponds?

True.

Maine has roughly 6,000 lakes and ponds.

Maine's official motto is "Dirigo." What does the word mean?

Dirigo is Latin for "I direct" or "I lead."

What city is the capital of Maine?

Augusta (population: 18,899).

Augusta was incorporated as a town in 1797 and as a city in 1849. The city is located on the Kennebec River at the head of the tide. It is the third least populated state capital in America.

Augusta has not always been the state capital. What other city once served as the capital of Maine?

Portland.

Portland served as Maine's capital city from 1820 to 1832.

What is the Maine state flower?

White Pine Cone and Tassel.

The White Pine Cone and Tassel (*Pinus Strobus Linnaeus*) was adopted by the legislature of 1895. The white pine is considered to be the largest conifer in the northeastern United States. Its leaves, or needles, are soft, flexible, and regularly grow in bundles of five.

How many counties are located in Maine?

16.

Countless Maine schoolchildren over the years have learned the names of the sixteen counties by memorizing the "Maine County Song." To what tune is that song sung?

"Yankee Doodle Dandy."

Name all sixteen Maine counties. No need to sing 'em.

Cumberland
Franklin
Piscataquis
Kennebec
Oxford
Androscoggin
Waldo
Washington
York
Lincoln
Knox
Hancock
Sagadahoc
Somerset
Aroostook
Penobscot

Seven of Maine's sixteen counties were founded after statehood in 1820. Name them.

Androscoggin
Aroostook
Franklin
Knox
Piscataquis
Sagadahoc
Waldo

What is Maine's smallest county when measured by land area?

Knox County.

It's only 374 square miles, but includes eighteen towns. In 2020 the population of the county stood at 40,607 and the county seat is Rockland. Knox County was named after Revolutionary War general Henry Knox.

Based on people per square mile, what is Maine's most sparsely populated county?

Piscataquis County.

Piscataquis County has a population density of 3.8 people per square mile. It has a land area of 4,378 square miles and a population of 16,800. Piscataquis County was created in 1838 from parts of Penobscot County and Somerset County and named for a Wabanaki word meaning "branch of the river."

In 2018, more than 1,000 people gathered at the fairgrounds in Skowhegan and did something for thirty seconds that later was officially recognized as a Guinness World Record.

Moose calling

Name the four Wabanaki tribes located in Maine.

Penobscot
Passamaquoddy
Micmac
Maliseet

What does *Wabanaki* mean in English?

People of the Dawn.

What do the letters "B" and "M" stand for in B&M Baked Beans?

Burnham & Morrill.

The company, founded by George Burnham and Charles Morrill, started canning meat, vegetables, and fish in when it opened in 1867. In 1913, B&M moved from its original location on Franklin Street in Portland to a new state-of-the-art cannery on Casco Bay. By the 1920s the company began experimenting with brick-oven baked beans to offset a decline in sales of other products. The product took off in the 1950s, during a post-war surge in bean sales.

In August 2021, the factory produced its last batch of old-fashioned beans. It was sold to a Falmouth-based non-profit and will eventually become home to Northeastern University's Roux Institute.

What is the state's official nickname?

The Pine Tree State.

Pretty straightforward, but it just sounds so much better than The Coffee Brandy State or The Scratch-Ticket State, which, according to legend, were two other suggestions.

What slogan began appearing on Maine license plates in 1936?

Vacationland.

What phrase became the official slogan of the state's tourism industry in 2012?

"Get lost!"

No, no, just kidding. It's really "Maine—the way life should be."

What do the initials "L.L." in L.L. Bean stand for?

Leon Leonwood.

In 2009, Linda Bean, granddaughter of L.L. Bean, teamed with Amato's to create the world's longest what?

Lobster roll.

It contained forty-five pounds of lobster meat and measured sixty-one feet and nine and a half inches.

A young Leon Leonwood Bean. Photo courtesy of Digicommons.

What is the official Maine pastime?

Going to yard sales.

Okay, we made that up; there is no official state pastime.

How many telephone area codes does Maine have?

One.

What is the state's area code?

207.

True or False: Maine is the only remaining state with just one area code?

False.

Maine is one of 11 states with a singular area code. The other states include New Hampshire and Vermont.

Where does the Maine Turnpike begin and end?

Kittery and Augusta.

While the official turnpike (dedicated in 1955) ends in Augusta, Interstate 95 continues to the Aroostook County city of Houlton on the Canadian border. The first section of the turnpike from Kittery to Portland was opened in 1947. At the time it opened, it was only the second long-distance superhighway in the United States.

True or False: Maine is larger in area than the other five New England states combined?

True.

At 33,215 square miles, Maine might seem small when compared to Alaska's 656,425 square miles, but it's still as large as the other five New England states—New Hampshire, Vermont, Massachusetts, Rhode Island, and Connecticut—combined!

What is Maine's highest mountain?

Katahdin (5,246 feet).

Katahdin overlooking Salmon Stream Lake. Photo by Shannon Butler.

Katahdin was designated as a National Natural Landmark in 1967. Katahdin is the centerpiece of Baxter State Park. It was named by the Penobscot tribe and means "Great Mountain."

Katahdin is the northernmost point of what famous trail?

The Appalachian Trail.

The southern terminus of the trail is Springer Mountain in Georgia. The trail passes through 14 states as it winds for roughly 2,200 miles from Georgia to Maine.

Where would you go in Maine for a bowl of Manhattan clam chowder?

Oh, please! This is a trick question.

There is no self-respecting place we know of—and certainly no place we would actually tell you about—that serves that kind of chowder in Maine. It's even named after Manhattan. In fact, Anna Crowley Redding in her delightful children's picture book, *Chowder Rules!*, recounts the noble effort by one state lawmaker to outlaw the use of tomatoes in clam chowder. So yes, we take this issue seriously.

True or False: More than 100 million pounds of lobster are caught in Maine each year?

False.

In 2022, an estimated 98 million pounds of the famous crustacean were caught off the coast of Maine. The total value of the catch was $388.6 million (not including butter and bib sales!) and the average price per pound paid to harvesters at the dock was $3.97. In the previous year, 108 million pounds of lobster were caught in Maine, meaning the catch decreased by about 10%. However, on a historic basis, the total catch is still near record highs when compared to previous decades. For example, in 1970 the catch was just 18.2 million pounds and in 1980 it was 21.9 million pounds.

Lobster fishing off the coast of Maine. Photo by WoodysPhotos | Shutterstock.

In 1791, the area that became Bangor was organized as a Plantation. What was it called?

Kenduskeag Plantation.

In 2002, Maine became the first state to give these devices to all seventh-grade students.

Laptop computers.

How long is Maine at its longest point?

About 310 miles.

The northernmost point is Big Twenty Township and the southern most point is Cedar Island in the Isle of Shoals.

Maine has only one syllable in its name. What other states also have only one syllable?

None.

What two professions are depicted on the Maine State Seal?

A Farmer and a Sailor.

Since there were no hipster baristas or Realtors back in 1820 when the seal was designed, designers went with a farmer on the left side of the seal and a mariner on the right—the two most common professions in the early nineteenth century.

What is the official state treat?

The Whoopie Pie.

Originally, the Whoopie Pie was going to be the state's official dessert, but the Big Blueberry Lobby didn't take kindly to that notion. And then, to further confuse matters, some lawmakers were concerned about glorifying a snack food given the growing issue of childhood obesity. So, the word "dessert" was changed to "treat," and the blueberry pie was designated the official dessert. Win-win!

What key ingredient differentiates a Maine frappe from a milk shake?

Ice cream.

What is Maine's official song?

The "State of Maine Song" by Roger Vinton Snow.

Snow won a state-song competition with this composition in 1931 and it was officially adopted by the Legislature six years later, on March 30, 1937.

Recite the lyrics to the "State of Maine Song":

Grand State of Maine,
proudly we sing
To tell your glories to the land,
To shout your praises till the echoes ring.
Should fate unkind
send us to roam,
The scent of the fragrant pines,
the tang of the salty sea
Will call us home.

CHORUS:
Oh, Pine Tree State,
Your woods, fields, and hills,
Your lakes, streams, and rockbound coast
Will ever fill our hearts with thrills,
And tho' we seek far and wide
Our search will be in vain,
To find a fairer spot on earth
Than Maine! Maine! Maine!

History

On what date did Maine officially become an independent state?

March 15, 1820.

Maine was admitted to the Union as the twenty-third state as part of what famous compromise?

The Missouri Compromise.

In 1820, Maine was admitted as a free state and Missouri was admitted as a slave state. The compromise was reached to appease southern politicians by maintaining a free-state, slave-state balance.

Prior to statehood, the so-called District of Maine was part of what other state?

Massachusetts.

Apparently, the people of Massachusetts were so upset at losing Maine land that they've been buying the state back one house lot at a time ever since.

In 1820, delegates from Maine's 236 towns met in Portland's First Parish Church to draft the required

state constitution. What name other than Maine was considered for the new state?

Columbus.

Statehood for Maine did not come quickly, or easily. In what year did Mainers first vote on whether to separate from Massachusetts?

May 1792.

It seems that after just a few short years under Massachusetts rule, Mainers threw up their arms and said, "Godfrey Daniel! And we thought the Brits were bad!" It was not until 1819, twenty-seven years later, that Mainers voted for a final time, approving separation, yet again. The final vote was 17,091 to 7,132.

What Portland native and powerful nineteenth-century national politician famously said about the two-party political system: "The best system is to have one party govern and the other party watch"?

Thomas Brackett "Czar" Reed.

Reed (1839–1902) served as Speaker of the U.S. House of Representatives from 1889 to 1891 and from 1895 to 1899. He was sometimes ridiculed as "Czar" Reed because of the tremendous power he had to control the agenda and operations of the House.

In 2022, this Portland woman became the first Black lawmaker elected as speaker of the Maine House of Representatives.

Rachel Talbot Ross

Ross, a ninth generation Mainer, is the daughter of Gerald Talbot, who was elected the first Black lawmaker in Maine.

In 1621, this Maine city became the first chartered city in America.

York.

First named Agamenticus, it was renamed Gorgeana in 1642 and then renamed York in 1652 when it became part of the Massachusetts Bay Colony.

The loss of this passenger steamer, with approximately 190 passengers and crew, is widely considered the worst maritime disaster in New England history.

The *Portland.*

The *Portland,* a 291-foot side-wheel paddle steamer, went down near Gloucester, Massachusetts in November 1898 during the Portland Gale, while making its regular run from Boston to Portland. The Portland Gale hammered the New England coast on November 26 and 27 in 1898. Overall, the storm killed an estimated 400 people and sank more than 150 boats and ships.

Passenger steamer SS *Portland* around 1885.

This famous clipper ship, launched in 1854, still holds the transatlantic speed record for sailing ships.

Red Jacket.

The *Red Jacket*, a clipper ship built at the George Thomas shipyard in Thomaston in 1854, is considered the fastest sailing ship in the world. She holds the transatlantic record for sailing ships, having sailed from New York to Liverpool—dock to dock—in thirteen days, one hour, and twenty-five minutes.

Who was Maine's first governor?

William King.

King (1768–1852)—a Bath merchant who is sometimes called the "Father of the State of Maine"—helped lead the movement that resulted in Maine's separation from Massachusetts.

General Ulysses S. Grant chose this Brewer native and Maine general to accept the sword of surrender from Robert E. Lee at Appomattox Court House in 1865.

Joshua Lawrence Chamberlain.

Chamberlain (1828–1914) is one of the most famous and important people in Maine history. He was the only officer during the Civil War to receive a battlefield promotion to general. He went on to serve as governor of Maine and president of Bowdoin College.

While accepting the sword of surrender from General Lee's army, what did Chamberlain famously tell his men to do?

Carry arms.

As defeated Confederate soldiers marched to surrender their arms and colors, Chamberlain ordered his men to come to

20

Col. Joshua Lawrence Chamberlain.

attention and "carry arms" as a show of respect. Chamberlain later described the scene: "All the while on our part not a sound of trumpet or drum, not a cheer, nor a word nor motion of man, but awful stillness as if it were the passing of the dead."

Bangor was known by what two nicknames in the nineteenth century?

Queen City of the East and Lumber Capital of the World.

Bangor became the nation's premier lumber town in the mid-1800s. The city is located at the head of the tide on the Penobscot River. Logs could be floated from the North Woods, processed into lumber, and then shipped around the world. By 1860, the city had 150 sawmills operating and more than 3,000 lumbering ships left its docks.

Every state has disorganized municipalities and governments, but Maine also has areas called "unorganized territories." Roughly how much of Maine is "unorganized"?

An estimated 44 percent.

The percentage of "disorganized places" is anybody's guess.

This high-flying 132-year-old Maine bank failed and was seized by FDIC regulators in February 1991. At the time, the failure was the largest and most costly bank failure in Maine history.

Maine Savings Bank.

What Maine man served as Abraham Lincoln's first vice president?

Hannibal Hamlin.

Hamlin (1809–1891), a native of Paris Hill, was a fiery politician and prominent U.S. senator who famously left the Democratic Party over its pro-slavery stance. He caused a national sensation when he joined the new Republican Party. He served as the first Republican vice president. For Lincoln's second term, politician Andrew Johnson—who was more sympathetic to the South—was chosen to replace Hamlin. Hamlin returned to the Senate for two six-year terms after he served as vice president.

Hamlin's vice presidency helped usher in a half-century of amazing national influence for the Maine Republican Party. Starting with Hamlin, Maine Republicans occupied the offices of vice president, secretary of the treasury (twice), secretary of state, president pro tempore of the United States Senate, and Speaker of the United States House of Representatives (twice). They also fielded a national presidential candidate in James G. Blaine.

In 1897, this person became the first registered Maine Guide.

Cornelia "Fly Rod" Crosby

What is the name of the Maine governor's mansion?

The Blaine House.

The house is the official residence of the governor of Maine, located on the corner of Capitol and State streets in Augusta.

For whom is Maine's governor's mansion named?

James G. Blaine.

Blaine (1830–1893), served in the Maine House of Representatives and the United States Congress. He was the Republican candidate for president in 1884, losing to Grover Cleveland. Blaine purchased the house in 1862 for his wife,

Hannibal Hamlin served as vice president of the United States under Abraham Lincoln. Photo courtesy of Library of Congress.

Harriet. Their daughter donated it to the state for a permanent governor's residence in 1919.

Fort Gorges, completed in 1864, was named after Sir Ferdinando Gorges who was a shareholder in the Plymouth Colony and helped fund the failed Popham Colony on the Kennebec River in Maine. What Maine city or town was the 56-gun fort built to protect?

Portland.

The two-story fort, modeled after Fort Sumter in South Carolina, remains a prominent feature in Portland Harbor, despite being labeled obsolete soon after its completion due to military advancements made during the Civil War.

Who was the last person executed in Maine?

Daniel Wilkinson.

On November 21, 1885, Wilkinson was hanged at Maine State Prison in Thomaston for the murder of a Bath police officer after an attempted burglary in the town. The death penalty was subsequently abolished in 1887.

This Hampden native was a nurse who helped change the way the mentally ill and handicapped are treated in America. She petitioned state legislatures to allocate money to create properly run mental institutions.

Dorothea Dix.

Dix (1802–1878) traveled to hospitals and prisons across the country and saw firsthand the deplorable manner in which the mentally ill and handicapped were treated, prompting her to take action. In addition, Dix served as the supervisor of nurses for the Union Army during the Civil War.

This Manchester native became an international sensation, capturing the hearts of the world when she wrote a letter to Soviet Premier Yuri Andropov in 1982 to express her fears about a possible nuclear holocaust.

Samantha Smith.

Following her letter, Andropov invited 10-year-old Smith (1972–1985) to visit the Soviet Union, making her one of our nation's youngest peace ambassadors. Smith and her father were killed in a plane crash in 1985. She was only 13 years old.

Where did the first Europeans settle in Maine?

On the St. Croix River.

In 1604, a French party, including Sieur de Monts and famed explorer Samuel de Champlain, settled on a small island in the river, midway between Maine and New Brunswick. It was a poor location. Half of the settlement died the first winter and the colony was abandoned.

Who named Mount Desert Island?

Samuel de Champlain.

As Champlain (1567–1635) was sailing past the island in the early 1600s, he looked at the island's barren mountains and called it *L'Isle des Monts-desert*.

Who was the first woman elected to the Maine House of Representatives?

Dora Pinkham.

Pinkham (1891–1941), a Republican school teacher and bookkeeper from Fort Kent, was elected in 1922.

Who were the first women elected to the Maine Senate?

Dora Pinkham and Katherine C. Allen.

Pinham, the same woman who was the first elected to the House in 1922, and Allen, a Republican and farmer from Hampden, were both elected to the senate in 1926.

In 1976, after a heated campaign, voters of Maine approved a referendum designed to reduce litter. By what name was the famous bill known?

The Bottle Bill.

The law, which required consumers to pay a deposit on soft drinks, beer, mineral water, and wine cooler containers, took effect in June 1978. It was later expanded to cover additional types of containers.

Alexander MacDonald, who co-founded the Maine Seacoast Mission in 1905, was inspired to serve the Maine islands after spending time working on this remote island fishing village in 1888.

Frenchboro, Long Island.

The Maine Seacoast Mission commissioned the first of its famous boats in 1912. What was its name?

Sunbeam.

The first *Sunbeam* brought books, supplies, church services, pastoral care, basic health care, and schooling to Maine islands and other isolated coastal communities.

In 2013, game warden Sargent Terry Hughes apprehended Christopher Knight, while Knight was breaking into a camp in Rome, Maine. Knight became

better known, both locally and across the nation, by what name?

The North Pond Hermit.

Knight survived as a hermit by committing an estimated 1,000 burglaries in the area.

According to some, which legendary European explorer may have actually been the first to visit Maine, around AD 1000?

Leif Erikson.

The Norse explorer is thought by some people to be the first European to set foot in what is now the continental United States.

Given the lack of actual evidence to support a visit to Maine by Vikings, who is identified as the first known European to explore the coast of Maine?

Giovanni da Verrazzano.

Verrazzano (1485–1528), an Italian explorer sailing for France, reached Cape Fear, North Carolina in 1524. He then sailed up the eastern coast of North America.

Where was the first British colony established in Maine?

The Popham Colony, in modern-day Phippsburg.

In 1607, just a few months after the more famous colony in Jamestown, Virginia, was established, Sir George Popham and his second-in-command, Raleigh Gilbert, established the Popham Colony. They arrived on the *Gift of God* in August, followed shortly by *Mary and John*. The 120 colonists built Fort St. George. A map made that October shows eighteen buildings. Roughly half of the colonists returned home that December, but the rest stayed the winter. Late the following summer of 1608, the entire colony returned to England. Apparently merry olde England looked a lot merrier after a Maine winter.

While the Popham Colony was short-lived, it is famous for what?

Building the *Virginia*, the first European-style vessel in America.

The thirty-ton pinnace was built at the mouth of the Kennebec River by the colonists of the unsuccessful settlement. They built the ship in part to prove the community could survive as a shipbuilding settlement. In the summer of 1608, when all the remaining colonists returned to England, some sailed on the *Mary and John* and the rest on the newly built *Virginia*. The *Virginia* would make at least one more transatlantic trip, helping to supply the Jamestown Colony in 1609.

In 1851, the so-called "Maine Law" was passed, making Maine the first state in the nation to ban the manufacture, sale, and possession of what product?

Alcohol.

The law was temporarily repealed in 1856, but essentially Maine was "dry" from 1851 until the 18th Amendment was repealed in 1933, ending Prohibition.

What famous Portland mayor was considered the "Father of Prohibition" and was the driving force behind the Maine Law?

Neal Dow.

Dow (1804–1897) was raised a Quaker and served as a city fireman and mayor of Portland. He even ran for president on the Prohibition Party ticket in 1880. He didn't win.

Not only was Neal Dow the force behind Prohibition, but he also served as a general during the Civil War. In fact, he was the highest-ranking Union officer ever to be held by the rebels. Eventually, he was exchanged for a relative of Robert E. Lee.

What Maine fort served as the staging ground for Benedict Arnold's failed attempt to attack Quebec in 1775?

Fort Western in Augusta.

Fort Western was built at the site of a 1628 Pilgrim trading post called Cushnoc. The fort was built during the French and Indian War in 1754. From 1754 to 1766 it was the site of a supply garrison to Fort Halifax. Today, the fort's main building has been restored to its original use as a trading post.

In 2022, who became the first Black man to serve on the Maine Supreme Judicial Court?

Rick Lawrence.

Lawrence, of Portland, was also the first Black man appointed to the bench in the state, becoming a district judge in 2000.

In what year was Maine's first newspaper published?

1785.

Benjamin Titcomb Jr. and his business partner Thomas B. Wait published the *Falmouth Gazette* and *Weekly Advertiser*. Interestingly enough, Marden's ran the first ad. Nah, just kidding; it was actually Reny's.

During the Revolutionary War, Portland was known by what name?

Falmouth.

After the war, a section of Falmouth known as the Neck grew rapidly as a commercial port. In 1786, the citizens of Falmouth Neck formed their own town and named it Portland.

In 1866, what famous poet looked out across a Portland devastated by fire and exclaimed: "Desolation! Desolation! Desolation! It reminds me of Pompeii."

Henry Wadsworth Longfellow.

Starting on July 4, 1866, a fire devastated Portland, destroying 1,500 homes, more than 100 manufacturers, and dozens of retail businesses and public buildings, including four schools. It left more than 10,000 people homeless.

The Great Fire of 1911 devastated the downtown section of what Maine city?

Bangor.

Flames engulf Bangor Savings Bank, the Bangor Public Library, and the Bangor Historical Society on April 30, 1911, along State Street in Bangor.

31

The Great Fire of 1911 wiped out nearly half of downtown Bangor. The fire burned fifty-five acres of the city, destroying 267 buildings and damaging 100 more. More than 260 buildings were completely gone, including six churches, a synagogue, the high school, the post office, the library, and the historical society. Dozens and dozens of businesses and homes were also destroyed.

In 1775, Captain Henry Mowat of the Royal Navy led a nearly twelve-hour bombardment of this Maine city, nearly destroying it.

Portland (Falmouth).

Capt. Mowat, of the 16-gun sloop HMS *Canceaux,* directed the bombardment of what is now Portland as punishment for the Battle of Machias. Mowat's flotilla included the 20-gun ship *Cat,* 12-gun schooner HMS *Halifax,* and the bomb sloop HMS *Spitfire.* But the time the bombardment ended, much of the city was destroyed, including its library, town hall, and Anglican Church.

In 1653, the "King's Highway" was built from Kittery to Portland and would eventually form the basis for what famed route?

U.S. Route 1.

The Crown Commissioners of Massachusetts ordered a road be built so they could hold court in the Province of Maine, spurring the road's initial construction.

What year were the first railroad tracks completed in Maine?

1836.

The tracks were completed by the Bangor and Piscataquis Canal and Railroad, and ran from Bangor to Old Town. This was the second railroad built in New England.

In what year did passenger train begin service in Maine?

1842.

In 1842, the Portland, Saco & Portsmouth Railway began service. The Boston-Maine Railroad arrived in 1843.

What was the connection between John Hancock—the famous signer of the Declaration of Independence—and York Village?

He owned Hancock Wharf.

The small eighteenth-century warehouse, and failed enterprise, is now acknowledged as the oldest known commercial structure in the state. It currently serves as a museum.

Where and when was Maine's first lobster pound located?

Vinalhaven Island, in 1875.

Maine has more than sixty lighthouses along its coast and islands. The first lighthouse commissioned by the federal government was Portland Head Light. Which U.S. president commissioned the famed lighthouse?

George Washington.

This lighthouse is located 21 miles offshore, further than any other lighthouse on the east coast.

Mount Desert Light.

Mount Desert Light is located on Mount Desert Rock, which is part of the town of Frenchboro. The current lighthouse was built in 1847 and was added to the National Register of Historic Places in 1988.

Mount Desert Light, located on Mount Desert Rock about 21 miles offshore. Photo by Dean Lunt

Where in Maine will you find the oldest surviving public building in the United States?

York.

The Old Gaol was built in 1719 and operated as a prison until 1879. It is now a museum and National Historic Landmark.

What Kennebunkport attraction bills itself as the world's oldest and largest museum of its type?

The Seashore Trolley Museum.

The collection, started in 1939 with the acquisition of a car from the Biddeford & Saco Railroad, features both stationary and working exhibits.

In 1775, the first naval battle of the Revolutionary War was fought off the coast near this town.

Machias.

On June 12, in what some call "The Lexington of the Seas," locals led by Benjamin Foster and Jeremiah O'Brien captured the British ship *Margaretta*, the first prize of the war. The *Margaretta* was refitted as a privateer. The ship's captain was fatally wounded during the battle while the crew was transferred to a prison near Boston.

Where was America's first veterans hospital located?

Togus.

It was founded in 1866 and is located just outside of Augusta. The campus is set on more than 500 acres, including both buildings and the natural landscape, and still operates as a nursing home and outpatient facility.

America's first sawmill was established in 1623 near what Maine town?

York.

What was the first town incorporated in Maine?

Kittery.

Incorporated in 1647, the original area of Kittery included today's towns of Eliot, South Berwick, Berwick, and North Berwick. It became part of the Massachusetts Bay colony after 1652.

Who or what were *Luther Little* and *Hesper*?

Schooners.

The *Luther Little* and *Hesper* were the names of the two four-masted schooners that sat, rotting, for years on the banks of the Sheepscot River in the town of Wiscasset, eventually becoming a tourist attraction.

Some say the folks of Wiscasset let them rot instead of trying to preserve them because both vessels were built in Massachusetts, which sounds plausible. They were only supposed to stay there until the shipping business got better, but then the Great Depression began, and by the time things improved the ships were beyond repair.

The Maine-built, 312-foot-long, four-masted, squared rigged transport bark *Dirigo* represented the first what built in the United States?

Steel-hulled ship

The *Dirigo* was launched from the Arthur Sewall & Co. shipyard in Bath in 1894. In 1917, during World War I, the *Dirigo* was torpedoed and sunk by a German submarine off the Irish coast.

When this man was elected governor in 1954, he was the first Democrat to hold the position in two decades, and when he was elected Maine's U.S. Senator in 1958, he was the first Democrat to hold that position in four decades. Who was he?

Edmund S. Muskie.

Muskie (1914–1996), of Rumford, was also United States Secretary of State under President Jimmy Carter and the Democratic Party's candidate for Vice President of the United States in the 1968 presidential election, alongside Hubert Humphrey.

What does the "S" in Edmund S. Muskie stand for?

Sixtus.

What schooner, built in 1871, is the oldest documented sailing vessel in continuous service in the United States?

Stephen Taber.

The schooner is a designated National Historic Landmark and is also part of the windjammer fleet that sails each week in the summer out of Rockland.

In 1976, the last river log drive in Maine took place on what river?

Kennebec River.

Environmental concerns and changing technology brought an end to the log drives, closing out a famous and remarkable era in Maine history.

Which Maine governor served the shortest time in office?

Nathaniel Haskell.

Haskell, of Pittsfield, served for just twenty-five hours in 1953. His short stint was the result of essentially a procedural issue following the 1952 elections. The sitting governor, Frederick Payne, who had been elected to the U.S. Senate, resigned early to prepare. Maine had no lieutenant governor, so the next in line was the President of the Senate, Burton M. Cross. As a result, Cross became the sitting governor. However, Cross was also the governor-elect and would no longer be a senator when his term ended. So, when his term in the senate officially expired on January 6, he could no longer be governor. At that point, Haskell was chosen as Maine's governor. But only until the following day, when Cross officially became governor, this time by virtue of his election the previous November. Got it? Politics can be so fun.

In 1969, Gov. Kenneth M. Curtis oversaw implementation of the first what in Maine history?

State income tax.

What U.S. vice president, although never a Maine resident, was born in Bar Harbor on July 8, 1908?

Nelson Aldrich Rockefeller.

Rockefeller (1908–1979) was governor of New York (1958–1973) and served as vice president under Gerald R. Ford (1974–1977). He was a summer resident of Seal Harbor on Mount Desert Island.

In 1953, what station became Maine's first television station?

WABI-TV.

The Bangor station, named after the WABI radio station, began broadcasting on VHF channel 5. The first full program was *Boston Blackie*, a detective drama about an ex-con turned private detective. Other early shows include *The Jack Benny Show* and *Your Hit Parade*.

What former Maine governor founded Community Broadcasting Services, the company responsible for putting WABI-TV, Maine's first television station, on the air?

Horace Hildreth.

Hildreth (1902–1988) was elected Maine's fifty-ninth governor in 1945. Two years later, he was reelected for a second term. However, in 1948, Hildreth lost the Republican nomination for

U.S. Senator to Margaret Chase Smith. In 1949, on the heels of that loss, the Gardiner native founded Community Broadcasting Services, which put WABI-TV on the air. Community Broadcasting Services later became Diversified Communications. From 1953 to 1957, Hildreth served the Dwight D. Eisenhower administration as U.S. Ambassador to Pakistan.

In 1862, Henry Franklin Morton founded the Paris Manufacturing Company in South Paris and became the first large-scale maker of what product?

Sleds.

Morton's family business employed almost 300 people in the early twentieth century, when each sled was made and painted by hand. The company eventually grew to become the largest and longest-running sled manufacturer in the country's history.

Speaking of things important in winter, what device was invented by John Alby Spencer of Island Falls?

The thermostat.

Sticking with the winter theme: What did Chester Greenwood, from Farmington, invent?

Earmuffs.

Each year on the first Saturday in December, Farmington hosts Chester Greenwood Day to celebrate the famous inventor.

What was the Stanley Steamer?

The Stanley Steamer was a lightweight transport vehicle powered by a steam engine that was wicked fast. The Steamer broke all kinds of speed records, some of which still stand today.

Who invented the Stanley Steamer?

Francis E. and Freelan O. Stanley.

Francis and Freelan were identical twins, born in 1849 in Kingfield. They were inventors, artists, violin makers, and all-around creative thinkers. They decided to try to build an automobile powered by steam, and built their first one, more or less from scratch, in 1897. Their company, the Stanley Motor Carriage Company, produced successful steam automobiles well into the 1920s.

The brothers also invented a procedure to develop photographs called a dry-plate process. They manufactured the equipment and eventually sold the Dry Plate Company (with headquarters in Lewiston) to George Eastman of Eastman Kodak.

Freelan, suffering from tuberculosis, moved to Estes Park, Colorado, where he built the now-famous Stanley Hotel in 1909. This hotel, listed on the National Register of Historic Places, is where Stephen King is said to have started writing *The Shining*.

Charles Forster of Strong, Maine is credited as the first person to mass-produce what product?

The toothpick.

Forster was the first to mass-produce and market what is probably the world's simplest and least-complicated device. No one has been able to create the digital version of the toothpick; it remains in its original analog form. Forster came in contact with toothpicks in South America, while he was a merchant seaman. He eventually started making them to sell when he quit the sea. His toothpick plant operated in Strong from 1860 until it closed in 2002.

Captain Hansen Crockett Gregory is the man most often credited with inventing what common and tasty treat?

The doughnut, or more specifically, the doughnut hole.

According to Earl H. Smith's book *Downeast Genius*, there are multiple stories of just how Gregory (1932-1921) came to invent the doughnut hole. The deep-fried pastry doughnut had been around for ages, having originated in the Middle East and eventually being brought to America by the Dutch. In the 1800s, Gregory was the captain of a lime ship that sailed out of his home port in Clam Cove, now the Glen Cove section of Rockport.

In one story, Gregory was sitting in the kitchen and asked his mother why the center of the fried cakes she was making were so soggy. She didn't know, so he took a fork and punched out the middle of the cut dough and asked her to fry that one. In another story, told later in life by Gregory, he was on a schooner eating fried cakes when he decided to take the ship's tin pepper box and cut out the tough middle.

In the most exciting version, Gregory was eating a dough- nut on June 22, 1847, when his ship was struck by a violent storm. In order to free both hands to manage the ship's wheel, he jammed his doughnut over one of the wheel spokes. When the calm seas returned, he reclaimed his impaled doughnut and discovered he had accidentally solved the long-held frustration of eating doughnuts with uncooked centers.

The exact details about the origin of the doughnut hole are scarce, but Clam Cove has a bronze plaque in town that immor- talizes Gregory and his tasty creation.

In 1995, Maine passed which controversial law intended to improve automobile safety?

The adult seat-belt law.

In 1965, Maine required that all passenger vehicles starting with the 1966 models be equipped with front-seat seat belts. In 1983, Maine required all children 4 and younger to sit in a child safety seat.

Who was the first woman to have her name placed into nomination for president by a major political party?

Senator Margaret Chase Smith.

In her remarkable career, Smith (1897–1995) was the first woman to serve in both houses of Congress, and the first woman to represent Maine in either. When asked by a reporter what she would do if she woke up one morning and found herself in the White House, Senator Smith's classic "Maine" answer was: "I'd apologize to Mrs. Eisenhower and go home." She is perhaps best known for her 1950 speech, "Declaration of Conscience," in which she criticized the tactics of Senator Joe McCarthy. She served as a U.S. Representative from 1940 to 1949, and as a U.S. Senator from 1949 to 1973.

What famous political family, which includes two presidents, has a summer home in Maine?

The Bush family.

George H.W. Bush was America's forty-first president and his son, George W. Bush, was the forty-third president. The Bush summer home is located on Walker's Point in the coastal town of Kennebunkport.

In the 1940s, a complex that came to be known as Camp Houlton, served what purpose?

Prisoner-of-war camp.

Camp Houlton operated from October 1944 to May 1946 at the former Houlton Army Air Base in Houlton. The camp housed more than 1,100 German prisoners-of-war, some of whom were allowed to work on area farms.

In 2019, which woman, born in Farmington, became the first female governor of Maine?

Janet T. Mills.

In 2013, Mills also became the first woman to serve as Maine's attorney general.

Nature & Wildlife

In less sophisticated areas, these pesky insects are sometimes called "buffalo gnats" or "turkey gnats." What are they called in Maine?

Blackflies.

Being a wholesome, family-oriented book, we won't include many of the earthy nouns, verbs, and participles used to describe the blackfly and the blackfly "experience." We've been told, but can't verify, that blackflies may have been first introduced into Maine as part of a government-sponsored program to help curb the burgeoning tourist population. However, not only do we now have more blackflies (and tourists) than ever before, but they also arrive earlier and leave later each year.

True of False: There are more than 10,000 species of insect in Maine?

True.

We don't blame you if you guessed "two"—the blackfly and the mosquito—but you're way off. On the other hand, if you've ever been camping in Maine and forgot the bug spray, you may have suspected that more than 16,000 distinct insect species make their home in Maine.

What is the Maine state bird?

Black-capped chickadee.

The black-capped chickadee is also the provincial bird of New Brunswick, which is fine, and the state bird of Massachusetts, which is kind of annoying.

Black-capped chickadee.

What is Maine's state insect?

Honeybee.

Yes, we've all heard the jokes about either the mosquito or the blackfly being our "official" state insect, but those stories are not true.

What is Maine's official fish?

Landlocked salmon.

The average landlocked salmon is sixteen to eighteen inches long and weighs one to one and a half pounds. However, it's not uncommon for a salmon to weigh three to five pounds. Prior to

1868, landlocked salmon were only found in four Maine river basins: the St. Croix, including West Grand Lake in Washington County; the Union, including Green Lake in Hancock County; the Penobscot, including Sebec Lake in Piscataquis County; and the Presumpscot, including Sebago Lake, in Cumberland County. Today, significant numbers of landlocked salmon can be found in more than 175 lakes and in more than 125 additional waters.

What two ocean currents meet thirty miles off the Maine coast?

The Gulf Stream and the Arctic Current.

True or False: The term "ice-out" signals that all ice has melted from the lake?

False.

The term "ice-out" doesn't mean that all the ice in the lake has melted; it just means that a boat can travel from one end of the lake to the other without being blocked by ice. Since they started keeping track, the earliest was April 14, in 1945. The latest date was May 29, in 1878.

What is the state berry?

Blueberry.

If you didn't say blueberry, Do Not Pass Go and return to Massachusetts immediately.

What percentage of the nation's wild blueberry supply is harvested in Maine?

98 to 99 percent.

Maine has more than 60,000 acres of wild blueberry fields. The majority of the state's blueberries are harvested in Washington County.

True or False: People in Maine see the sun rise before anyone else in the country?

True.

The exact location depends on the season. In winter, the top of Cadillac Mountain is the first to see the sun. Folks in the Aroostook County town of Mars Hill claim they see the sun first from mid-March to mid-September. And folks in Lubec say that right in between, at the spring and fall equinoxes, you can see the sun first at West Quoddy Head, the peninsula that is the easternmost part of Maine.

What is the easternmost point of land in the United States?

West Quoddy Head.

West Quoddy Head is in Quoddy Head State Park in Lubec. In 1808, a lighthouse was constructed there to guide ships through the Quoddy Narrows. The current tower, which is red-and-white striped, was built in 1858.

What is Maine's largest island?

Mount Desert Island.

At 108 square miles, MDI, as it's known locally, is the second-largest island along the nation's East Coast and the sixth-largest island in the contiguous United States. Long Island, New York is the largest island on the East Coast, while Hawaii is the largest in the United States overall. Home to Acadia National Park, more than 4.1 million tourists visit MDI each year. Meanwhile, the year-round population is only about ten thousand. That is a remarkable ratio.

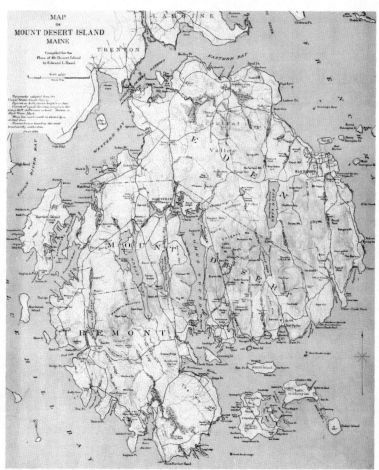

Mount Desert Island. Map courtesy of Library of Congress.

Name Maine's five highest mountains.

1. Katahdin (5,246 feet)
2. Sugarloaf (4,237 feet)
3. Old Speck (4,180 feet)
4. Crocker Mountain (4,168 feet)
5. Bigelow Mountain (4,150 feet)

What is the state herb?

Wintergreen.

Wintergreen was adopted as Maine's state herb by the legislature in 1999. The low-growing plant produces white blooms in the summer and red berries in the winter. It is often used to flavor tea, gum, and toothpaste.

What is the state gemstone?

Tourmaline.

Mount Mica, located near Paris in Oxford County, was the first source of tourmaline in the United States, and became the first gem mine in America as well. Mount Mica was discovered in 1821 by two young men walking through the area, Ezekiel Holmes and Elijah Hamlin. Elijah Hamlin, later one of the founders of Bangor Savings Bank, was the brother of Hannibal Hamlin, who would serve as Abraham Lincoln's first vice president.

What is the state tree?

Eastern white pine.

This pine can grow from 75 to 150 feet tall. The white pine helped establish Maine as the lumber capital of the world in the nineteenth century and as the nation's predominant shipbuilding state.

True or False: More than 80 percent of Maine land is covered by forest?

True.

The state is nearly 90 percent forested. Maine has an estimated 17.52 million acres of forest land. At the height of its lumber industry, only 53 percent of the state was covered in forest.

What is the state animal?

Moose.

A moose can grow up to seven feet tall at the shoulder and can weigh more than 1,500 pounds. A typical moose lives fifteen to twenty-five years. Many consider the moose part of the Holy Trinity of Maine tourism, which are: the moose, the lobster, and the lighthouse.

An adult moose in winter. Photo by Harry Collins Photography | Shutterstock.

What is Maine's largest lake?

Moosehead Lake (74,890 acres).

Sebago Lake (28,771 acres) is a distant second, followed by Chesuncook Lake (23,070 acres). Located in northwestern Maine's Piscataquis County, Moosehead is home to over eighty islands and is the source of the Kennebec River.

In what month does the average daily high temperature in Maine exceed 80 degrees?

Seriously? This. Is. Maine. The answer is none.

What is the longest river in Maine?

The St. John River (418 miles).

However, the St. John River—which forms the northern boundary between Maine and Canada—is not entirely in Maine. The state's second-longest river, and the longest river located entirely in the state of Maine, is the Penobscot River, which, including the river's west and south branches, is 264 miles long.

What Maine seabird is known as a "Sea Parrot"?

Atlantic puffin.

The Atlantic puffin (*Fratercula arctica*) is a species of seabird in the Auk family. It is the only puffin native to the Atlantic Ocean.

True or False: A lobster can be either left-handed or right-handed?

True.

Each lobster has a larger crusher claw and a smaller pincher claw. The crusher claw is used to break up hard food such as clams and crabs, while the pincher claw is used to tear apart softer prey such as worms or fish. These claws can be on different sides of a lobster's body, as the crusher claw is always on the lobster's dominant side.

True or False: If a lobster loses one of its claws, it can grow a new one?

True.

Lobster traps and buoys on Frenchboro, Long Island. Photo by Dean Lunt.

If a lobster loses a claw, antenna or leg, it is able to grow it back. It typically takes about five years for a lobster to regenerate a claw that is the same size as the one it lost.

Although some adult males can grow to weigh as much as 600 pounds, how much does a typical newborn bear cub weigh?

About twelve ounces.

How much could that same bear cub weigh at the end of its first summer?

About seventy-five pounds.

And that's mostly from a diet of Maine blueberries, so if you're watching your weight, be careful with those blueberries. (Just kidding!)

True or False: More than 400 different species of birds have been spotted in Maine?

True.

The most common backyard birds in the state include: American Crow, Black-capped Chickadee, American Goldfinch, Blue Jay, and Song Sparrow.

What is the fastest bird found in Maine?

Peregrine Falcon.

The falcon can hit speeds of more than 200 miles per hour during a hunting dive. Peregrine Falcons were nearly extinct in the eastern United States by the mid-1960s, primarily due to pesticides, but have made an amazing comeback.

What is the lightest bird found in Maine?

The ruby-throated hummingbird.

This migratory hummingbird checks in at 0.11 ounces.

Other than the fact that it has a lot of beavers, what is a key reason that Maine has a lot of beaver dams?

It is illegal to disturb a beaver dam.

Although their dams can flood roads, destroy crops, and kill trees in low-lying areas, beavers are an important species in the Northeast, as they create habitats for other wildlife species, including fish and many aquatic plants.

Maine has no poisonous snakes, but we do have some large snakes that can become unpleasant if cornered or captured. What is the largest snake found in Maine?

The black racer.

These snakes can grow to be six feet in length. The name "racer" is apt because they are very fast and will flee from danger. If cornered they can get downright ugly, and will bite. The snakes can also rattle their tails in dry leaves to impersonate rattlesnakes. If you capture one, be prepared for it to writhe, defecate, and spray musk all over you. Or, you could just leave it alone.

What is considered the largest member of the deer family?

Moose.

A mature male can weigh up to 1,500 pounds, which would be considered large in any family. This is why the moose shops in the Deer Big & Tall shops when it needs a new flannel shirt.

What is the state cat?

Maine coon.

The large and friendly Maine coon is one of the oldest natural breeds in North America. Its size, dense fur, raccoon-like tail, and other features help the breed survive Maine's harsh winters.

In September 1954, these two famous hurricanes struck Maine just 12 days apart, causing millions of dollars in damage and killing at least eight people.

Hurricane Carol and Hurricane Edna.

What does the Wabanaki word "musquash" refer to?

Muskrat.

The muskrat's name comes from two scent glands near its tail that give off a strong "musky" odor, which the muskrat uses to mark its territory. Aren't you glad we humans have advanced to things like surveyor's stakes to mark our territories?

How does the snowshoe hare camouflage itself?

Its fur changes color.

In the winter their fur is snow white, but in the summer and fall it's rusty brown.

Let's slow things down here with a question about turtles. What three species of marine turtles are found in the Gulf of Maine?

Leatherback, loggerhead, and Kemp's ridley (also called Atlantic ridley).

The leatherback and loggerhead are some of the largest marine turtles; the Kemp's ridley is one of the smallest of marine turtles. All three are endangered species, so just leave them alone, okay?

Speaking of the Gulf of Maine, what are its eastern and western boundaries?

To the west, Nantucket Shoals, just off Massachusetts; to the east, Cape Sable Island, the southernmost point of Nova Scotia.

What four species of owls are most commonly found throughout Maine?

Barred, great horned, northern saw-whet, and eastern screech.

It's hard to say which is the wiser.

True or False: Maine has the largest concentration of Moose in the United States?

False.

Alaska holds that distinction with Maine coming in second. Maine state biologists estimate the Maine moose population to be around 70,000.

Between 1997 and 2010, this famous tree in Yarmouth, stood 110 feet tall and was the oldest and largest elm tree in New England. What was its given name?

Herbie.

While the beloved tree, which was planted in the 1770s, was felled in 2010, its "ancestors" live on. The Liberty Tree Society, of Walpole, New Hampshire, offers seedlings derived from Herbie's DNA.

What did some of Maine's first English settlers call whales?

Sea hogs.

We're sure the whales would have called the settlers worse if they could have.

How many years has the great blue heron (considered the world's greatest fisherman) been visiting the Maine coast?

More than forty million years.

That is the estimate based on fossils that have been found. However, great blue heron are not native to the area. They're seasonal visitors, so they're still considered "from away," and even though they're hatched here, their offspring are not considered native either.

What do Down East families make with "tips" and "boughs"?

Christmas wreaths.

What is the specific purpose of a weather stick?

Predicting rain.

Yes, we're serious. Weather sticks are made from balsam fir or birch rods. They point up in low humidity and down in high humidity. Do they work? Well, a good weather stick has as good an average as your average TV weatherman or -woman, and doesn't need computers, satellite feeds, or any of the other digital gizmos modern meteorologists use.

In 1816, Mainers saw snow in June and frost in both July and August. What is the common nickname for that year?

Eighteen Hundred and Froze to Death.

It was also known as the Year Without a Summer. The disastrously low temperatures, most likely caused by a massive volcanic eruption in Indonesia, caused a worldwide food shortage.

On average, what is Maine's warmest month?

July.

The average high in Portland in July is 77 degrees.

On average, what is Maine's coldest month?

January.

The average low in Portland is 5 degrees. The average low in Caribou is 0 degrees.

How many miles of the famed Appalachian Trail are in Maine?

281.

And the trail ends (or starts, depending on how you look at it) atop Maine's highest point, Mount Katahdin.

Who or what is Pamola?

The mythical protector of Katahdin.

According to Wabanaki mythology, Pamola has the head of a moose, the body of a man, and the wings and claws of an eagle.

With a wingspan of just 1.5 inches, what endangered species can be found only at the top of Katahdin?

Katahdin arctic butterfly.

The Katahdin arctic is a subspecies of the *polixenes arctic*, which inhabits in the arctic tundra from Alaska through northern Canada to Labrador. However, the Katahdin arctic is not found anywhere else in the world other than the summit of Katahdin. It is illegal to collect or possess this butterfly.

The first national park created east of the Mississippi is located in Maine. Can you name it?

Acadia National Park.

Located on a rocky shore in Bar Harbor that is inaccessible at high tide, this cave and natural bridge was once thought to be an entrance to the underworld. What is it called?

Devil's Oven.

The Devil's Oven can be viewed from the water by kayak, or hiked to at low tide. The sea cave was once one of Acadia's largest attractions, but has since been removed from maps and signage as several visitors became trapped inside by the rising tide.

The Devil's Ovens rock formation along the shore in Bar Harbor is among the dozens of places in Maine associated with names Devil and Hell. Photo courtesy of Earl Brechlin.

Which Portland native and former state representative, state senator, and governor donated the 202,064 acres of land now known as Baxter State Park to the state?

Percival Baxter (1876–1969).

Baxter, a Portland-native, was the fifty-third governor of Maine (1921-1925). He was a leader in the effort to acquire land and create the state park.

What percentage of Maine blueberries are sold fresh?

Less than 1 percent.

In 1999, the 972-foot-long Edwards Dam was removed from this river, opening spawning grounds to salmon that had been blocked for 162 years.

Kennebec River.

On July 1, 1999, the Edwards Dam, built in 1837, became the first such structure in the United States to be dismantled against the wishes of its owner.

This Brunswick woman, a botanist and artist, produced the influential book, *Flora of Maine*. (Hint: She also discovered two plants that are named after her.)

Kate Furbish (1834-1931)

Furbish worked on *Flora of Maine*, a collection of paintings and sketches of Maine's flowering plants, from 1870 to 1908. The original work contains 1,326 watercolors and sketches. The plants named after Furbish are: Furbish lousewort (*Pedicularis furbishiae*) and heart-leaved aster (*Aster cordifolius var. furbishiae*)

Sports

What Cheverus High School graduate won five Olympic medals in swimming, including three gold, one silver, and one bronze?

Ian Crocker.

Crocker, who was born in 1982, competed in the Olympic games three times—in 2000, 2004, and 2008.

Maine's Ian Crocker was the first swimmer to break fifty-one seconds in what swimming event?

The 100-meter butterfly.

He improved this world record twice, before it was broken by Michael Phelps in 2009.

What Hampden Academy graduate was named to the 2000 American League All-Star team as a shortstop? (Hint: He replaced the legendary Cal Ripken as the shortstop for the Baltimore Orioles in 1997.)

Mike Bordick.

Bordick played for four major league teams from 1990 to 2003, amassing 1,500 hits and compiling a .260 career batting average. He played in one World Series for the New York Mets.

The University of Maine won the National Championship in 1993 and 1999 in what sport?

Men's ice hockey.

Who coached Maine's two national-championship hockey teams?

Shawn Walsh.

Walsh (1955–2001) had a career coaching record of 399-215-44. In 1992-1993, he led Maine to a 42-1-2 record and its first national championship, after defeating Lake Superior State of Michigan. When he took over as the Maine coach in 1984, the team's record the preceding three years was 27-65. He died in 2001 at the age of 46 after a battle with cancer.

The University of Maine hockey team plays its home games in the Alfond Arena. For whom is the arena named?

Harold Alfond.

Alfond (1914–2007) founded the Dexter Shoe Company and established the first factory outlet store. Alfond and his family, through the Harold Alfond Foundation, have donated tens of millions of dollars to charitable causes, helping to build several college athletic stadiums and fields.

What graduate of South Portland High School and the University of Maine led the National League in Earned Run Average while pitching for the San Francisco Giants in 1992?

Billy Swift.

Swift, who won a silver medal while pitching for the United States in the 1984 Olympics, also won twenty-one games that year. For his major league career, he was 94-78, with a 3.95 earned run average.

This former baseball player for the University of Maine was named World Series MVP in 2022 after helping the Houston Astros win the World Series.

Jeremy Peña

Peña, who played shortstop and batted .400 during the series, was the first rookie position player to be named World Series MVP. He was also named MVP of the American League Championship Series, becoming the first American League player to win both awards in the same year. The Astros selected Peña in the third round of the 2018 draft.

Two Maine sports medicine professionals treated what team at the 2022 Winter Olympics in Beijing?

The U.S. women's ice hockey team.

Dr. Allyson Howe, a family and sports medicine doctor at InterMed in South Portland, served as the team physician. She was joined by Wayne Lamarre, the director of the University of New England's athletic training program.

Cape Elizabeth-born Joan Benoit was the first woman to ever win what sporting event?

The women's Olympic marathon.

Benoit won the gold medal at the 1984 Summer Olympics in Los Angeles, the year that the women's marathon was introduced.

While her claim to fame was as an Olympic marathon champion, what sport did Joan Benoit first play at Cape Elizabeth High School?

Field hockey.

Joan Benoit founded a 10-kilometer race along the coast of her hometown, from Crescent Beach State Park to Portland Head Light. What is it called?

Beach to Beacon.

The race began as a local event in 1998 with 3,000 runners and has since doubled in size. Athletes from throughout the country, and the world, now participate in the annual event. In 2009, online registration for the race filled up in just 1 hour and 45 minutes.

What Maine resident was crowned the first Olympic Snowboard Cross Champion?

Seth Wescott.

Wescott, who lives in Carrabassett Valley, won the inaugural event at the 2006 Winter Olympics in Torino, Italy.

Bert Roberge pitched for the University of Maine and played six years in the major leagues for three teams. Name them.

The Houston Astros, Chicago White Sox, and Montreal Expos.

The Lewiston native played mostly as a reliever and compiled a 12-12 career record, with a 3.98 Earned Run Average (ERA).

Who is the only boxer from Maine to win a world boxing title?

Joey Gamache.

Gamache, of Lewiston, won not just one but two world boxing titles—the WBA Super Featherweight title in 1991 and the WBA Lightweight title in 1991. Just be advised: Don't call Joey a "lightweight."

In 1965, Muhammad Ali famously fought what heavyweight boxer for the title at St. Dominic's Arena in Lewiston?

Sonny Liston.

On May 25, 1965, Ali (then known as Cassius Clay) defeated Liston in one minute and twelve seconds of the first round.

What forgetful singer sang a tortured version of the National Anthem at the Clay-Liston heavyweight bout in Lewiston?

Robert Goulet (1933–2007).

Best known for his portrayal of Lancelot in *Camelot* on Broadway, Goulet made headlines for flubbing the lyrics to the *Star-Spangled Banner*.

Who was known as the "Deerfoot of the Diamond"?

Louis Sockalexis.

Sockalexis (1871-1913), a member of the Penobscot tribe, is said to have been the first Native American to play in the major leagues. He played in the national league for the Cleveland Spiders from 1897 to 1899.

What Portland native and member of the Boston Red Sox Hall of Fame was a first-round pick of the Red Sox in 1974? (Hint: his nickname was "The Steamer").

Bob Stanley.

Stanley pitched only for the Red Sox during his thirteen-year major league career, compiling a 115-97 career record, while recording a Red Sox record of 132 saves. He is the only pitcher to register at least 100 wins and 100 saves with the Red Sox.

What Cherryfield right-handed pitcher was named National League Pitching Rookie of the Year by the *Sporting News* in 1958?

Carlton Francis Willey.

Willey (1931-2009) pitched eight years in the major leagues for the Milwaukee Braves and New York Mets. As a rookie, he pitched in the 1958 World Series against the New York Yankees. He finished with a lifetime 38-58 record and career ERA of 3.76.

What Lawrence High School and University of Maine basketball star was a first-round draft pick of the Cleveland Rockers of the Women's National Basketball Association (WNBA) in 1998?

Cindy Blodgett.

Blodgett, while playing for the Maine Black Bears, led the nation in scoring for two consecutive seasons, averaging more than twenty-seven points per game in her sophomore and junior years. At Lawrence, her teams were 84-4 and won four state championships.

What Newburgh native and 1995 NASCAR Winston Cup Rookie of the Year won the closest finish in NASCAR Sprint Cup series history?

Ricky Craven.

In 2003, Craven won the Carolina Dodge Dealers 400, beating Kurt Busch by 0.002 seconds, or mere inches. (In 2011, the record was tied at the Aaron's 499 when Jimmie Johnson beat

University of Maine star player Cindy Blodgett readies for a foul shot during and exhibition game at Alfond Arena in Orono. Photo by David MacDonald; courtesy of the Portland Press Herald.

Clint Boyer by the same margin.) Maine's Craven finished his career with two Sprint Cup wins and forty-one top ten finishes. After he retired, Craven was a broadcaster with ESPN.

What St. Albans native began his major league baseball career in 1898 with the Brooklyn Bridegrooms?

George Henry Magoon.

Magoon (1875-1943) played for five major league teams in his five-year career as a shortstop and second baseman, finishing his career with a .239 batting average and driving in 201 runs. But the real question is, the Brooklyn Bridegrooms? Yes, the Bridegrooms. You may recognize them better by their present name—the Los Angeles Dodgers. The Bridegrooms were also known through the years as the Grooms, Superbas, Robins, and Trolley Dodgers. They became the Brooklyn Dodgers in the 1930s.

Dick MacPherson (1930-2017), former head coach of the Syracuse Orange football team and the New England Patriots football team, is a native of what Maine town?

Old Town.

At Syracuse University, he compiled a record of 66-46-4, including one undefeated season in 1987. His overall college coaching record was 111-73-5. He was inducted into the College Football Hall of Fame in 2009. The New England Patriots were 8-24 during his tenure. He inherited a team that had finished 1-15 in 1990.

This woman played basketball for Gorham High School and Indiana University, and was named a first-team All-American by the Associated Press in 2023.

Mackenzie Holmes

What Washington County native and former major league baseball player is credited as the baseball scout who signed Jackie Robinson?

Clyde "Sukey" Sukeforth.

Sukeforth (1901–2000) played for the Cincinnati Reds and the Brooklyn Dodgers. He was a manager in the Dodgers farm system before his promotion to Leo Durocher's Dodgers staff in 1943, where he served as both coach and scout.

Sukeforth was the only other person in the room when Dodgers president Branch Rickey told Robinson of his plans to sign him to a contract to play in Montreal in 1946. Because Durocher was suspended for two games in 1947, Sukeforth actually managed Robinson's first major league game. Sukeforth turned down an offer to serve as manager for the 1947 team, which went on to win the National League Pennant. Later, Sukeforth followed former Dodgers General Manager Branch Rickey to the Pittsburgh Pirates organization. There, as a coach and scout, he played a role in the Pirates' drafting of Roberto Clemente from the Dodgers' organization. He later turned down an offer to manage the Pirates. Sukeforth died in Waldoboro in 2000.

The painting titled "Game Called Because of Rain" is one of Norman Rockwell's most famous works. It appeared on the cover of The Saturday Evening Post, published April 23, 1949. Sukeforth is the Brooklyn player in the painting.

Another sidenote; in 1951, when Dodgers manager Chuck Dressen needed a reliever to face the New York Giants' Bobby Thomson in the ninth inning of the decisive third game of the National League pennant playoff, Sukeforth, coaching in the Dodgers' bullpen, passed over Carl Erskine and sent in Ralph Branca, who gave up Thomson's "shot heard 'round the world."

Bangor Daily News sportswriter Bud Leavitt appeared in a series of television commercials for J.J. Nissen bread with what legendary baseball player?

The Splendid Splinter himself, Ted Williams.

In what ballpark does the Double-A Portland Sea Dogs baseball team play its home games?

Hadlock Field.

For whom is Hadlock Field named?

Edson B. Hadlock Jr.

Hadlock (1923–1984) was a long-time Portland High School baseball coach and physics teacher and is a member of the Maine Baseball Hall of Fame.

Speaking of the Portland Sea Dogs, the team is now associated with the Boston Red Sox organization. What major league team was the original parent of the Sea Dogs?

Florida Marlins.

What Colby College graduate won thirty-one games for the Philadelphia Athletics in 1910, while setting an American League record for most shutouts in one season?

John "Jack" Coombs.

Coombs (1882–1957) also won three games in the 1910 World Series when Philadelphia beat the Chicago Cubs. Coombs finished his career with a 158-110 record and went on to coach the Duke University baseball team for more than twenty years. Both the Duke and Colby baseball fields are named after Coombs.

Before the Portland Sea Dogs, what was the name of Maine's most recent minor league baseball team?

Maine Guides.

The Guides were a AAA team that played at Old Orchard Beach and were an affiliate of the Cleveland Indians.

Lobster fisherman Edmund "Rip" Black (1905-1996) of Bailey Island won the bronze medal in the 1928

Olympics in Amsterdam in what event? (Hint: He often used this in his day job).

The hammer throw.

What Lewiston native, nicknamed "Rough," was a catcher-manager for the Boston Red Sox, guiding the team to the World Series championship in both 1915 and 1916?

William "Bill" Carrigan.

Carrigan (1883–1969) also played on the 1912 team that won the World Series and was elected to the Boston Red Sox Hall of Fame. Babe Ruth reportedly called Carrigan the best manager he ever played for.

In what event did Robert LeGendre, a two-time Olympian from Lewiston, win a bronze medal at the 1924 Olympic Games in Paris?

The pentathlon.

In the process of winning that medal, LeGendre (1898–1931) set the world record for the long jump. His jump as part of the pentathlon was longer than the jump that won the gold medal in the actual long jump event.

What Portland bowler was twice world singles champion in candlepin bowling and twice named Bowler of the Year? (Hint: She was also the first woman inducted into the Maine Sports Hall of Fame.)

Dorothy "Dot" Petty.

Petty's candlepin bowling career spanned more than twenty years and included 84 titles and 16 records. The Portland native was Pro Tour Bowler of the Year in 1977, 1978, 1982, and 1983.

What University of Maine baseball coach guided the Black Bears to the College World Series six times?

John Winkin.

Overall, ninety-two of Winkin's former players signed professional baseball contracts. Winkin (1919-2014) was elected to eleven halls of fame, including the National Baseball Hall of Fame.

Biddeford native Freddy Parent played shortstop for the 1903 Boston Red Sox. What is that team most famous for doing?

Winning the first Major League World Series.

Freddy Parent (1875–1972) played in the major leagues for eleven seasons and was mostly known for his defense, although he finished with a career batting average of .262. When he died in Sanford in 1972, he was the last surviving member of the first World Series championship team.

How many Portland Sea Dogs headed to the 2021 Olympic Games in Tokyo?

Twelve current and former Sea Dogs.

Four current Sea Dogs, including Tiston Casas, Joe Meneses, Ronaldi Baldwin, and Denyi Reyes, and eight former players participated in the 2021 Olympic Games. Four players represented Team USA, while the others represented Mexico, Dominican Republic, and Israel.

Arts & Literature

Author Stephen King is closely associated with the city of Bangor, although he was actually born in Portland. However, he grew up in neither. From what Maine high school did King graduate?

Lisbon Falls High School, class of 1966.

What college did Stephen King attend?

The University of Maine at Orono.

King graduated with a BA in English, in 1970.

At what Maine high school did Stephen King teach English?

Hampden Academy.

In the movie *Shawshank Redemption*, based on a novella by Stephen King, Tim Robbins's character tells Morgan Freeman's character to visit a hayfield in what Maine town, to find a special package?

Buxton.

Who described Maine in these words?

"All I could see from where I stood
was three long mountains and a wood
I turned and looked the other way
and saw three islands in a bay."

Award-winning poet and Camden native Edna St. Vincent Millay in "Renascence."

What Pulitzer Prize-winning humor writer suggested that Maine's actual state motto should be: "Cold, but damp!"?

Dave Barry.

Barry is an author and longtime syndicated columnist for the *Miami Herald.*

What is the name of the character played by Tim Robbins in the *Shawshank Redemption*?

Andy Dufresne.

What Pulitzer Prize–winning historical novel, which focused primarily on the four days of the Battle of Gettysburg, is credited with reviving interest in the heroics of Joshua Lawrence Chamberlain and the 20th Maine Infantry Regiment at Little Round Top?

The Killer Angels by Michael Shaara.

The book was awarded the Pulitzer Prize for Fiction in 1975. One key scene in the book is Chamberlain's defense of Little Round Top on the second day of the battle. Confederate forces sensed weakness at that point and began attacking the Union left flank. Chamberlain and the 20th Maine were sent to defend the southern slope of Little Round Top at the far left end of the entire Union line.

The small hill held extreme strategic significance, and Chamberlain knew the 20th Maine had to hold the Union left at all costs.

The 15th Alabama Infantry Regiment repeatedly attacked Chamberlain's position until the 20th Maine was almost doubled back upon itself. With many casualties and ammunition running low, Chamberlain ordered his left wing to initiate a bayonet charge. The 20th Maine charged down the hill, with the left wing wheeling continually to make the charging line swing like a hinge, thus creating a simultaneous frontal assault and flanking maneuver, capturing 101 of the Confederate soldiers and successfully saving the flank.

Speaking, again, of Stephen King: The movie *Firestarter*, starring Drew Barrymore, had its world premiere in what Maine city?

Bangor.

On May 9, 1984 the Bangor Opera House, formerly the Bangor Cinema, hosted King, 9-year-old Drew Barrymore, and the rest of the crew.

Which Portland native wrote several series of popular books set in Maine that were aimed at middle school boys, including the Elm Island series and the Whispering Pine series?

Elijah Kellogg.

Kellogg (1813-1901), a famous minister at churches in Harpswell and Topsham, began writing children's books in the 1860s after attending Bowdoin College and the Andover Theological Seminary.

Which Portland native created such magazines as *Ladies' Home Journal* and *The Saturday Evening Post?*

Cyrus Hermann Kotzschmar Curtis.

Curtis (1850-1933) founded the eventual publisher of these magazines, Curtis Publishing, in 1891.

Maine native and Westbrook High School graduate Kevin Eastman created what famous comic book and animated characters?

The Teenage Mutant Ninja Turtles.

In 1984, Eastman and collaborator Peter Laird spent $1,200 to self-publish the first edition of *The Teenage Mutant Ninja Turtles* in black and white.

In the television series Seinfeld, Kittery-native John O'Hurley starred as this recurring character?

Jacopo Peterman.

Referred to as J. Peterman, or simply Peterman, he is the owner of the J. Peterman Catalog Sales Company and is Elaine's eccentric boss during her employment there.

Portland-area musician Dave Gutter co-wrote the song "Stompin' Ground," which won a GRAMMY in the Best American Roots performance category in 2023. Who performed the song?

Aaron Neville

What Portland native earned a nomination for the Academy award for Best Supporting Actress for her role in *Up in the Air*? (Hint: She earlier gained fame for her role in The Twilight Saga).

Anna Kendrick.

Kendrick, who attended Deering High School, began her career on Broadway, starring in the musical *High Society* at 12 years old. She also starred in the box-office hit series *Pitch Perfect.*

Which famous artist said, "Never put more than two waves in a painting"?

Winslow Homer.

Homer (1836-1910) moved to Prouts Neck in 1883, where he painted monumental sea scenes.

In the movie *Forrest Gump,* the title character played by Tom Hanks spends more than three years running around America. When he reaches the Atlantic Ocean in New England, what lighthouse is he shown visiting?

Marshall Point Lighthouse in Port Clyde, Maine.

Who founded the *Portland Press Herald*?

Guy Patterson Gannett.

Gannett (1881-1954) purchased the *Portland Daily Press* and the *Portland Herald* and merged them to create the *Portland Press Herald* in 1921. In 1925, Gannett also purchased the *Portland Evening Express, Daily Advertiser,* and the *Portland Sunday Telegram.*

What firm designed the Portland Museum of Art?

I.M. Pei & Partners

The museum, founded by the Portland Society of Art in 1882, is the largest and oldest pubic art institution in the state. It used a variety of different exhibition spaces until Charles Shipman Payson donated $8 million, along with his collection of 17 Homer paintings, toward a new building to be designed by Henry Nichols Cobb of I. M. Pei & Partners. Construction began in 1981 and the museum opened its doors within the next two years.

For whom is Rockland's Farnsworth Museum named?

William A. Farnsworth

Farsnworth (1815–1876) was a successful Rockland businessman. His daughter Lucy Farnsworth (1838–1935) directed that the bulk of the Farnsworth estate be used to establish the William A. Farnsworth Library and Art Museum as a memorial to her father. The museum officially opened in August 1948.

Which Fort Fairfield native recorded the huge country hit, "Tombstone Every Mile," which climbed to Number 5 on the Billboard charts in 1965?

Richard "Dick" Curless.

Curless (1932–1995) was known as the Baron of Country Music and a pioneer of the trucking music genre. Curless recorded twenty-two songs that appeared on the Billboard Charts, including "Big Wheel Cannonball." In the late 1960s he toured with the legendary Buck Owens.

In the song, "Tombstone Every Mile," Dick Curless says if you're haulin' goods in Maine, you'd rather be anywhere else but where?

Dick Curless, 1984. Photo by John Ewing; courtesy of Portland Press Herald.

The Hainesville Woods.

Staying on topic, can you recite the refrain from "Tombstone Every Mile"?

It's a stretch of road up north in Maine
That's never, ever, ever seen a smile
If they buried all the truckers lost in them woods
There'd be a tombstone every mile
Count 'em off, there'd be a tombstone every mile.

Which Maine humorist and singer starred in the Maine Public Broadcasting show called *In the Kitchen*?

Kendall Morse.

Morse (1934–2021) was inducted into the Maine Country Music Hall of Fame in 1995 and was nominated for a Grammy in 2009. He was also named Maine Folksinger of the Year three times and wrote the popular book *Father Fell Down the Well.*

Who wrote the now-classic book of Maine humor, *A Moose and a Lobster Walk into a Bar . . .*

John McDonald.

Hey! We know, shameless!

Which two fictional Maine fishermen popularized the saying, "You can't get there from here"?

Bert and I.

Which two Yale students created "Bert and I"?

Marshall Dodge and Robert Bryan.

Dodge (1935–1982) and Bryan (1931–2018) cut the first "Bert and I" album in 1958. Filled with exaggerated Yankee accents and bone-dry comedy, the records elevated folk story-telling to an art form in Maine and beyond, inspiring the likes of Tim Sample, Joe Perham and Kendall Morse.

Marshall Dodge, co-creator of the Bert and I stories, emerged as the leading Maine humorist of his generation. Photo courtesy of Islandport Press.

In the original Bert and I story, what was the name of the duo's boat?

The *Bluebird*.

In the 1970s, Marshall Dodge starred in a television show that aired on Maine Public Broadcasting. Name the show.

A Downeast Smile-In.

Who is widely acknowledged as President Lincoln's favorite humorist?

Charles Farrar Browne.

Browne (1834–1867), a Waterford native, adopted the pen name Artemus Ward and achieved great popularity in America and England. In fact, before unveiling "The Emancipation Proclamation" to his cabinet, Lincoln read Ward's "Outrage at Utica," which is said to have outraged some of the humorless members of his Cabinet. Ward also inspired Mark Twain. Ward died of tuberculosis while on a tour of England in 1867 when he was thirty-three.

Mary Nelson Archambaud, who appeared in the 1930 movie, *The Silent Enemy*, was a writer, chorus line dancer, and performer of traditional Native American dances in the United States and Europe. She is better known by what name?

Molly Spotted Elk.

Molly Spotted Elk was a member of the Penobscot Nation and was born on Indian Island. Her parents were Horace Nelson, a Penobscot political leader, and Philomene Saulis Nelson, an artisan basket maker.

In what fictional Maine town was the popular television show, *Murder, She Wrote* set?

Cabot Cove.

The supposedly quiet New England town seemingly had the highest murder rate per capita in the country. Thank goodness for Jessica Fletcher or things would really have gotten out of hand!

From what fictional town did the character Hawkeye Pierce from the movie and television show, M*A*S*H, hail?

Crabapple Cove.

In 1972, Richard Hooker, author of *MASH: A Novel About Three Army Doctors* on which the movie was based, wrote a sequel called *M*A*S*H Goes to Maine*. In the book, Hawkeye returns to Crabapple Cove, which is located near Spruce Harbor.

The famous poet Edwin Arlington Robinson was born in Alna in 1869 and was raised in this town, which served as a model for his famous "Tilbury Town" poems.

Gardiner.

What popular American folk band from Portland take their name from a hero of the Revolutionary War whose place in history was cemented by legendary Portland poet Henry Wadsworth Longfellow?

The Ghost of Paul Revere

The trio, including Max Davis, Sean McCarthy, and Griffin Sherry, made their national debut as the musical guest on a talk show hosted by Conan O'Brien in 2018. In April 2022, the band announced that they would be disbanding. Their final performance took place in September of that year at Thompson's Point in Portland.

Which famous Maine humorist wrote a weekly column for the *Christian Science Monitor* for more than sixty years and penned the popular book *Farmer Takes a Wife*?

John Gould.

Gould (1908–2003) wrote from a farm in Lisbon Falls and later from Friendship. He also wrote thirty humorous books about Maine.

Which writer said he found Maine's woods, "moosey and mossy"?

Henry David Thoreau (1817-1862).

Thoreau, a naturalist, poet, and essayist, wrote *The Maine Woods*, which chronicles three trips into the backwoods of Maine in 1846, 1853, and 1857. He is best known for his classic book *Walden*.

Cape Elizabeth native Sean Aloysius O'Fearna is better known by what name?

John Ford.

Ford (1894–1973), a legendary filmmaker, graduated from Portland High School and soon headed west to make movies. He directed more than eighty films and won four Academy Awards for Best Director. He was perhaps best known for his westerns, which included *Stagecoach* and *The Searchers*, both starring John Wayne. He won an Academy Award for directing John Steinbeck's *The Grapes of Wrath*.

Which well-known nineteenth-century American author spent his teenage years living in Raymond and later attended Bowdoin College, where he was a classmate of future president Franklin Pierce and poet Henry Wadsworth Longfellow?

Nathaniel Hawthorne

Hawthorne (1804–1864) wrote *The Scarlett Letter* and *The House of the Seven Gables*.

Which former contributor to *The New Yorker* moved to North Brooklin, Maine, where he wrote classic children's books?

A. Elwyn Brooks, better known as (E. B.) White.

White's (1899–1985) books include *Charlotte's Web, Stuart Little,* and *The Trumpet of the Swan.*

In E.B. White's classic *Charlotte's Web*, which is set in Maine, what is the name of the pig?

Wilbur.

What play, set in Veazie, and written by Maine native Owen Davis, won the 1923 Pulitzer Prize for Drama?

Icebound.

The play opened on Broadway on February 10, 1923 and closed on June 1, 1923 after 145 performances. It was also made into a film of the same name, directed by William C. deMille in 1924.

Which artist, noted for his large-scale paintings inspired by the deep woods of Maine, lived in Lincolnville?

Neil Welliver.

Although Welliver (1929–2005) was born in Pennsylvania and studied at the Philadelphia College of Art and Yale, he permanently settled in Lincolnville in 1970.

Who painted "Christina's World," one of the best-known paintings in American history?

Andrew Wyeth.

Where is the house depicted in "Christina's World" located?

Cushing.

The house is known as the Olson House. The woman featured in Wyeth's famous painting is Christina Olson, who was stricken with Charcot-Marie Tooth (CMT) disease, a disease that paralyzed her lower body. Wyeth was inspired to create the painting when, through a window from within the house, he saw her crawling across a field.

What is the name of the novel inspired by "Christina's World"?

A Piece of the World by Christina Baker Klein.

Which Brunswick native and Rhodes Scholar wrote "Strange Holiness," which won the Pulitzer Prize for Poetry in 1936?

Robert P. Tristram Coffin.

Coffin (1892–1955), a Bowdoin College professor with degrees from Bowdoin, Princeton, and Oxford, wrote more than three dozen books of literature, poetry, and history.

Which Portland-born nineteenth-century poet was considered the most influential poet of his day, writing such classics as "Evangeline," "The Courtship of Miles Standish," and "Paul Revere's Ride"?

Henry Wadsworth Longfellow

Longfellow (1807-1882) grew up in what is now known as the Wadsworth-Longfellow House on Congress Street in Portland and attended Bowdoin College.

Which Rockland native won the Pulitzer Prize for Poetry in 1923 for "The Ballad of the Harp-Weaver"?

Edna St. Vincent Millay.

Millay (1892–1950) a lyrical poet, playwright, and noted feminist, was the first woman and second person to win the distinguished award.

Which former Colby College professor and current Camden resident received the 2002 Pulitzer Prize for Fiction for his Maine-based novel *Empire Falls*?

Richard Russo.

Which Alna native, raised in Gardiner, won the Pulitzer Prize for Poetry three times and was nominated for the Nobel Prize in Literature four times?

Edwin Arlington Robinson.

Robinson (1869–19535) first won the Pulitzer in 1922 for his first *Collected Poems*. In 1925 he won for *The Man Who Died Twice*, and then in 1928 for *Tristam*.

Which Kennebunk-native and former *Saturday Evening Post* writer won a Pulitzer Prize Special Citation "for his historical novels which have long contributed to the creation of greater interest in our early American history"?

Kenneth Roberts.

Roberts' (1885–1957) works include *Arundel, Rabble in Arms,* and *Northwest Passage.*

What popular Maine performer is better known as the lead character from her play, *Ida: Woman Who Runs with the Moose?*

Susan Poulin.

Poulin has authored two books, *The Sweet Life* and *Finding Your Inner Moose: Ida LeClair's Guide to Livin' the Good Life*, as well as ten plays, five of which feature her alter ego, LeClair. Susan also writes the popular Maine humor blog and podcast "Just Ask Ida."

Performer Susan Poulin as her alter ego, Ida LeClair. Photo courtesy of Islandport Press.

What son of Westbrook starred in the original Broadway production of *How to Succeed in Business without Really Trying*?

Rudy Vallée .

Vallée (1901–1986) was offered the part of J. B. Biggley after British actor Terry Thomas turned it down.

According to legend, President Abraham Lincoln reportedly said this upon meeting this Maine author: "So you are the little woman who wrote the book that started this great war"?

Harriet Beecher Stowe.

Stowe (1811–1896) wrote *Uncle Tom's Cabin* and published it as a serial in the weekly anti-slavery journal *The National Era*.

Harriet Beecher Stowe wrote *Uncle Tom's Cabin* while living in what Maine town?

Brunswick.

At the time, Stowe lived with her family in Brunswick where her husband taught at Bowdoin College. The home is now a protected National Historic Landmark.

In 1997, this band drew more than 75,000 people to a concert on the former Loring Air Force Base in Limestone.

Phish.

On August 17, Phish closed out The Great Went concert festival. Their tens of thousands of fans briefly made Limestone the most heavily populated town in Maine.

What member of the 1960s trio, Peter, Paul and Mary, lives in the Hancock County town of Blue Hill?

Noel Paul Stookey.

He was the trio's "Paul."

Stookey first recorded his solo albums in a four-story henhouse on his Maine property. This studio, also known as "The Henhouse," was the origin point of what radio station's first broadcasts?

WERU-FM.

The station signed on the air on May 1, 1988. Stookey was the station's first benefactor. In 1997 the station moved to its current location in East Orland.

What legendary rock star famously died just days before he was scheduled to perform at the Cumberland County Civic Center?

Elvis Presley.

The King (1935 –1977) was scheduled to perform in Portland on August 18, 1977, but he died of heart failure on August 16.

What Buckfield native and Bowdoin College graduate created the character Major Jack Downing and is credited with being one of the first humorists to use American vernacular in humor?

Seba Smith.

Smith (1792–1868) was a newspaper editor and humorist who some consider the father of Down East humor, because of his dry, satirical style. He influenced subsequent humorists, including Artemus Ward.

A movie poster for *Deep Waters*, based on the novel *Spoonhandle* by Ruth Moore.

This Blue Hill native wrote the novel *Silas Crockett*, considered one of the most important books in Maine history.

Mary Ellen Chase.

Chase (1887–1973) wrote more than thirty novels set on the Maine coast including *Mary Peters* and *Windswept*. Her summer home in Steuben, where she lived in from 1941 to 1955, inspired *Windswept*.

Author Elizabeth Ogilvie set her most popular novels on what fictional Maine island?

Bennett's Island.

Ogilvie (1917-2006) wrote more than forty novels, including the Tide Trilogy: *High Tide at Noon, Storm Tide,* and *The*

Ebbing Tide, all set on Bennett's Island, inspired by the real-life island of Criehaven located in outer Penobscot Bay.

The 1948 film *Deep Waters* was filmed on location in Vinalhaven and nominated for an Academy Award. The movie is based on *Spoonhandle,* a New York Times-bestselling book written by what Maine author?

Ruth Moore.

Moore (1903–1989), born on Gotts Island, also wrote *The Weir, Candlemas Bay,* and other novels set on the Maine coast. The financial success of *Spoonhandle* allowed Moore to build a house in Bass Harbor and spend the rest of her life writing.

What actor, born in Lewiston and raised in Buckfield, starred as neurosurgeon Dr. Derek Shepherd on the television show *Grey's Anatomy*?

Patrick Dempsey.

His *Grey's Anatomy* character was written as a graduate of Bowdoin College after an alumnus started a petition that was signed by over 450 other students.

What did Patrick Dempsey found in 2008 as a response to his mother's journey with ovarian cancer?

The Patrick Dempsey Center.

The center, with locations in Lewiston and South Portland, provides support services to cancer patients, survivors, care partners, family members, and friends at no cost.

Maine native David E. Kelley, a famous television and film writer whose first film script was *From the Hip* starring fellow Maine native Judd Nelson, is married to

which famous actress? (Hint: She starred in the movie *Scarface*.)

Michelle Pfeiffer.

What Portland native starred in the 1980s movies *St. Elmo's Fire* and *The Breakfast Club*?

Judd Nelson.

What Portland native appeared in the TV show *Barney Miller* and starred as Alice Hyatt on the TV sitcom *Alice*? (Hint: She also won a Tony for her performance in Neil Simon's *Broadway Bound*.)

Linda Lavin.

Although she had been performing since the age of five, Lavin attended Waynflete in Portland before going on to study at the College of William and Mary.

What Lewiston artist is considered one of America's best modernist painters, who painted some of his most famous works—including *Evening Storm* and *Lobster Fisherman*—while living in Maine?

Marsden Hartley.

Hartley (1877–1943) died in Ellsworth at the age of sixty-six. His ashes were scattered along the Adroscoggin River.

Author John N. Cole (1923–2003), author of *In Maine*, co-founded this influential weekly newspaper with Peter Cox in 1968.

The Maine Times.

The Maine Times kept watch on government activity and chased stories other newspapers were ignoring, but it was ground-breaking in its focus on environmental reporting.

Portland-native Victoria Rowell rose to prominence starring as Drucilla Winters on what famous soap opera?

The Young & the Restless.

For her role as Winters, Rowell was nominated for three Daytime Emmy Awards. In addition to many other roles, Rowell also played Dr. Amanda Bentley in the CBS medical crime drama *Diagnosis: Murder*.

In 2019, NASA astronauts Jessica Meirs and Christina Koch were the first women to participate in an all-female spacewalk. What Maine high school did Meirs, who was also included in *Time* magazine's 100 Most Influential People of 2020, graduate from?

Caribou High School.

This 1999 movie, based on a novel by John Irving, was set in Maine and stars Tobey Maguire, Charlize Theron, and Paul Rudd. Some scenes for the movie were shot on Mount Desert Island.

The Cider House Rules.

Scenes for what 1957 movie, based on the then-shocking and sensational novel by Grace Metalious of the same name, were shot in Belfast, Camden, and Rockland?

Peyton Place.

The movie starring Lana Turner, Hope Lange, and Diane Varsi, was released in December 1957. It was nominated for nine Academy Award, while the book spent 59 weeks on the *New York Times* best seller list. The world premiere of the movie took place at the Camden Theater on Mechanic Street. The movie was shot largely in Camden and hundreds of local residents were hired as extras to appear in the movie.

Which legendary movie actress who called herself the "Yankee-est gal who ever came down the pike" was born in Massachusetts, but in the 1950s she owned a home and lived in Cape Elizabeth with her husband, Gary Merrill, and their children?

Bette Davis.

As a teenager, Davis worked as Ogunquit's first female lifeguard. She returned to Maine in 1986 to film scenes on Cliff Island for one of her final movies, *The Whales of August*.

Clarence White, who was born in Lewiston as Clarence Joseph LeBlanc, was an American bluegrass and country guitarist and singer. In the late 1960s, he was a member of what rock band?

The Byrds.

The band, formed in Los Angelos in 1964, helped pioneer the folk rock genre by melding the influence of British bands like the Beatles with contemporary and traditional folk music.

Which Old Town-born folk singer and songwriter won two Grammy Awards?

Patty Griffin.

Griffin won her first Grammy in 2011 for Best Traditional Gospel Album, and her second in 2020 for Best Folk Album.

Maine Places

What Maine city is known as the City of Ships?

Bath.

Thomas W. Hyde (1841–1899), a Civil War general and Medal of Honor recipient, founded this famous business on the coast of Maine.

Bath Iron Works.

What is the most visited tourist spot in Maine?

Acadia National Park.

More than 4 million people visited Acadia in 2021, making it one of the 10 most popular national parks in the United States.

In the 1930s, the world's largest yacht was built at Bath Iron Works for J. P. Morgan. Can you name it?

Corsair IV.

The *Corsair IV*, which means "pirate" or "pirate ship" was the largest yacht built in the United States. The *Corsair IV* is said to have cost J. P. Morgan $2.5 million. And those, of course, were 1930s Depression-era dollars. In 2022 dollars, the value would be more than $44 million.

Otter Cliff in Acadia National Park. Photo by Dean Lunt.

True or False: Augusta is the second easternmost state capital?

False.

Augusta is *the* easternmost capital city in the United States.

The yacht *Ranger* was built at Bath Iron Works for Harold S. Vanderbilt, great-grandson of Cornelius Vanderbilt. What is *Ranger's* greatest claim to fame?

Winning the 1937 America's Cup.

Ranger beat challenger *Endeavour II* from England. After winning the cup, *Ranger* was hauled out and never raced again. It was sold for scrap in 1941, for $12,000.

How do many residents of Portland refer to the city's two main sections?

"Place with many coffee shops" and "place with fewer coffee shops." No, seriously, Portland's two distinct areas are "on-peninsula" and "off-peninsula."

In what Maine town was America's first sardine cannery built?

Eastport.

The first U.S. sardine cannery opened in Eastport in 1875, when a New York businessman set up the Eagle Preserved Fish Company.

By what name was Bangor supposed to be called?

Sunbury.

According to legend, settlers sent Reverend Seth Noble to Boston to name their town Sunbury, but for some reason he changed his mind along the way and named it Bangor, after his favorite Irish hymn. He and his fellow townspeople were obviously not singing from the same hymnal.

Which River does the Sarah Mildred Long Bridge span?

Piscataquis.

The Sarah M. Long Bridge is a lift bridge that carries Route 1 traffic across the Piscataquis River, which serves as the border between New Hampshire and Maine. The bridge was named in honor of Sarah Mildred Long, who was an employee of the Maine–New Hampshire Bridge Authority for more than fifty years.

What are the easternmost and westernmost points in Maine?

West Quoddy Head in Lubec to the east and the town of Lebanon in the west.

The distance between the two is about 152 miles east to west.

Where is Maine's most famous cribstone bridge?

Bailey and Orr's islands.

Both islands are located in the town of Harpswell.

What five rivers meet in Merrymeeting Bay? ("Meet"—get it?)

Kennebec, Androscoggin, Cathance, Abagadasset, and Eastern.

As they say in Brunswick, the more rivers, the merrier the meeting.

In 1799, this sixth Maine county became the first one in the state that did not have any seacoast.

Kennebec County.

What is the most overused place name in Maine?

Mud Pond.

This name wins dirty hands down with sixty-five. But the muddy fun doesn't end with ponds. Maine also has twelve Mud Brooks and fourteen Mud Lakes. Those names would suggest that there's a lot of mud here in Maine—and indicate a lack of originality in our state's Department of Place Names.

What is the more commonly known name for Portland's Morse-Libby House?

Victoria Mansion.

The building was constructed between 1858 and 1860 as a summer home for Ruggles Sylvester Morse and his wife Olive. After Morse's death, Olive sold the house to J.R. Libby, a dry goods merchant. While the Libby family made a few changes to the property, they also preserved the original furnishings and occupied the Mansion until 1929.

In 1860, this Maine county became the state's sixteenth and final county. (Hint: It is created from parts of existing Lincoln and Waldo counties.)

Knox County.

Name the northernmost community in Maine and New England.

Estcourt Station.

Estcourt Station, Maine is a tiny village in Big Twenty Township. While there are logging roads into town, Estcourt Station has no public roads that connect it to Maine. Travelers must travel into Canada, then cross into the village by using a public road. Estcourt Station is located at the southern end of Canada's Lake Pohenegamook. According to legend, a giant sea monster named Ponik inhabits the lake and flips over boats to eat the passengers.

Rachel Carson, who wrote *Silent Spring*, which is often credited with kicking off the modern environmental movement, was a summer resident of what Maine island?

Southport Island.

Name Maine's five largest cities, in terms of population. Bonus points if you can name them in order from largest to smallest.

Portland (65,645)
Lewiston (36,583)
Bangor (32,403)
South Portland (25,280)
Auburn (23,639)

What is Maine's smallest city in terms of population?

Eastport (1,274).

Eastport, located in Washington County, was incorporated as a city in 1893. The city reached a peak population of 5,311 in 1900.

Who named Christmas Cove?

Explorer John Smith.

Smith (1580–1631) anchored in the cove of the Damariscotta River on Christmas Day in 1604 and decided to name the quaint cove after the day.

Eastport was once considered The Capital of the World for what industry?

Sardines.

In the late nineteenth century, Eastport boasted thirteen large sardine-canning factories operating twenty-four hours a day, seven days a week, during the season. Today, there are no canning operations in Eastport.

What U.S. road, laid out in the 1920s, stretches from Fort Kent at the northern tip of Maine all the way to Key West, Florida?

U.S. Route 1.

The border town of Fort Kent is named for the fort built there on the Maine-Canadian border. The fort and the town are named for Edward Kent, a Maine governor.

What Maine village is considered the highest in the state?

Paris Hill.

Paris Hill is 831 feet above sea level—as high as any Maine town ought to be. The historic village was Oxford County's first shire town, and the birthplace of Hannibal Hamlin, Abraham Lincoln's first vice president. The Hamlin Memorial Library and Museum is housed in what was the Oxford County jail.

This Portland building is the oldest African-American church building in Maine and the third-oldest in the United States.

Abyssinian Church.

Because of its easy access by rail and sea, Portland became a northern hub of the Underground Railroad in the 1800s. The Abyssinian Church played a critical role in providing safe houses and finding escape routes to Canada and England. It was added to the National Register of Historic Places in 2006.

Eden was the original name of what Maine town?

Bar Harbor.

The film, The Man Without a Face was primarily shot in what Midcoast town?

Camden.

The Man Without a Face, starring and directed by Mel Gibson, was based on Isabelle Holland's 1972 novel of the same name. The movie was released in 1993.

From what Maine town did the first transatlantic balloon flight begin?

Presque Isle.

Double Eagle II, piloted by Ben Abruzzo, Maxie Anderson, and Larry Newman, became the first balloon to cross the Atlantic Ocean in 1978, when it landed in Miserey, France, near Paris, after a flight of 137 hours and 6 minutes.

What river was Fort Knox built to protect?

The Penobscot River.

Even as late as 1844, it was felt that a fort was needed on the river to protect the Penobscot River Valley from a British naval attack. The fort was made from granite cut from nearby Mount Waldo.

What is the nickname for Aroostook County?

The County.

At 6,453 square miles, not only is it Maine's largest county, but it's also larger than Connecticut and Rhode Island combined. Granted, there may be only a few places smaller than Lil' Rhody, but Aroostook's size is still pretty impressive.

Potato fields in Aroostook County. Photo by Shannon Butler.

The airport code for the Portland Jetport is PWM. What do the initials PWM stand for?

The Portland-Westbrook Municipal Airport.

L.L. Bean was founded in Freeport in 1912 and has become synonymous with Maine. What original product is credited with building the Bean empire?

The Maine Hunting Shoe.

In the movie *The Preacher's Wife*, starring Whitney Houston and Denzel Washington, in what Maine park was the ice-skating scene filmed?

Deering Oaks Park in Portland.

Where is the last active Shaker community in the United States?

Sabbathday Lake, in New Gloucester, Maine.

Established in 1783 at the height of the Shaker movement, the community had two remaining members as of 2022.

From what Maine town did the granite come to build the monument to General Ulysses S. Grant on Riverside Drive in New York City?

North Jay.

Granite from Vinalhaven Island was shipped to New York to build the towers and approaches of this famous bridge.

Triborough Bridge.

The Triborough Bridge, (Now called the Robert F. Kennedy Bridge) links the boroughs of Manhattan, Queens, and the Bronx.

How many granite quarries were being worked in Maine at the end of the nineteenth century?

More than 100.

On what mountain range does the Appalachian Trail cross into Maine?

The Mahoosuc Mountains.

The Mahoosuc range is a northern extension of the White Mountains that crosses over from New Hampshire northwest of Bethel, near where Route 26 does.

What historic prep school is located in the western town of Bethel?

Gould Academy.

What was Maine's first college?

Bowdoin College.

The college, located in Brunswick, was chartered in 1794, and classes commenced in 1802. The charter was signed by Massachusetts Governor Samuel Adams.

For whom is Bowdoin College named?

James Bowdoin II (1726-1790).

Bowdoin, a former Massachusetts governor, was an investor in the Kennebec Purchase Company, a large landowner in Maine. James Bowdoin III arranged for the establishment of Bowdoin College in the name of his father.

In 1813, the Commonwealth of Massachusetts established the Baptist-influenced Maine Literary and Theological Institution, which became better known as what school in 1899? (Hint: In 1871, it became the first

all-male college or university in New England to accept female students.)

Colby College

What ski resort did Les Otten purchase in the mid-1980s and build into one of New England's most popular ski destinations?

Sunday River.

Located in Newry, the resort has the most terrain among the East Coast skiing destinations, including eight peaks.

What town was flooded and destroyed in 1949, when Central Maine Power Company dammed the Dead River? (Hint: The state's fourth largest lake has the same name.)

Flagstaff.

The town of Flagstaff was abandoned and dismantled (and legally disincorporated) in 1950 to allow construction of a hydroelectric dam on the Dead River, which enlarged Flagstaff Lake and submerged the site of the settlement.

The Garmin office building in Yarmouth is home to the largest of these in the world. What is it?

A globe.

The globe, named Eartha, weighs approximately 5,600 pounds and has a diameter of over 41 feet.

What Seal Harbor summer resident built the sprawling 100-room "cottage" named Eyrie in 1912? (Hint: Think Standard Oil.)

John D. Rockefeller.

Rockefeller (1839–1937) and his family summered at the house on Mount Desert Island for decades, until the family demolished it in 1962.

What Maine Seacoast town is the area that was named Megunticook by the Wabanaki?

Camden.

Schooners in Camden Harbor. Photo by Dean Lunt.

Famous gangster and bank robber Al Brady was killed in an FBI ambush outside of Dakin's Sporting Goods Stores in the downtown of what Maine city?

Bangor

Brady, 26, and an accomplice were killed on October 12, 1937. Brady is buried in an unmarked grave in Bangor's Mount Hope Cemetery.

The Maine Maritime Museum is built on the site of what famous Kennebec River shipyard?

Percy & Small.

Built in 1894, the shipyard was originally comprised of five buildings, including a carpenter shop, paint shop, caulking shed, a mould loft, and a building containing a generator. It is now the only surviving shipyard site where large wooden sailing vessels were built in America.

The sailing vessel *Wyoming* was built at Percy & Small in 1909 at a staggering $175,000. What is its claim to fame?

The *Wyoming* is the largest wooden sailing vessel ever built.

The ship was 450 feet from jib boom to spanker boom tip. The *Wyoming* was equipped with a state-of-the-art Maine-built Hyde windlass to haul it, a massive anchor, and a donkey steam engine to haul and lower its sails. The donkey engine allowed the *Wyoming* to be sailed with a smaller crew of only eleven hands.

Because it was so long and made of wood, the *Wyoming* tended to flex in heavy seas. The flexing caused the long planks to twist and buckle, which allowed seawater to pour into the hold—something all sailors know is never good. Her crew had to use pumps to keep its hold as free of water as possible. In March 1924, the *Wyoming* foundered in heavy seas and sank off Cape Cod with the loss of all hands.

For whom is Bath's Carlton Bridge named?

Frank W. Carlton.

The state senator from Woolwich introduced legislation to fund the bridge in 1925. How badly did the people in the Bath area want to replace the ferry with a modern bridge? Well, the vote on the referendum question to issue the state bonds to pay for the span was 2,800 "yes" votes to 103 "no" votes. Although named for Senator Carlton, the original idea for the bridge came from Luther Maddocks of Boothbay Harbor.

In 1965, the city of Portland officially created "One Beanpole Circle" as the home address for which iconic Maine company?

B & M Company.

The company, founded in 1867, was famous for its baked beans.

What Maine lighthouse enjoys the distinction of being the smallest lighthouse officially registered with the U.S. Coast Guard?

Pocahontas Light.

Pocahontas Light, located on Echo Point on Great Diamond Island in Casco Bay, stands only six feet tall.

Which of Maine's 64 lighthouses is the tallest?

Boon Island Light.

The lighthouse, built on a rock ledge, is six miles off the York coast and stands 133 feet tall. It was built in 1811 and then replaced in 1851. The tallest lighthouse in America is Cape Hatteras Lighthouse, Outer Banks, North Carolina, which stands 200 feet tall.

True or False: Maine has more than 2,500 offshore islands?

True.

Maine actually has more than 4,000 offshore islands, although only 1,200 are larger than one acre in size.

Lunt Harbor in Frenchboro, Maine. Photo by Dean Lunt.

Which unbridged Maine island has the largest year-round population?

Vinalhaven.

Located about twelve miles off Rockland, Vinalhaven has a population of 1,269. The second largest island is Peaks Island, which is part of Portland, with more than 900 year-round residents. Islesboro is the third largest with nearly 600 residents.

On what Maine river did the Americans suffer a naval defeat so devastating that it would stand as the nation's worst naval disaster until Pearl Harbor?

The Penobscot River.

The Penobscot Expedition was the largest American naval expedition of the American Revolutionary War. In 1779, British forces began establishing a fortification in what is now Castine. That July, an American force, which boasted 19 armed ships mounting 344 guns and 24 transports, and more than 1,200 men, began attacking the British. However, the Americans were ultra-cautious and essentially laid siege by not pressing the attack.

In mid-August, the Royal Navy reinforcements arrived. The American fleet initially massed to fight, but then turned and fled up the Penobscot River, where they were pinned. The entire American fleet was either sunk by the British or scuttled by the Americans themselves. The men fled into the woods. Those who survived traveled through dense wilderness back to Boston. Overall, the Americans lost 43 ships and approximately 500 men.

Final Round

This Kennebunk house, built for shipbuilder George W. Bourne in 1825, was once called "the most photographed house in Maine." What is its nickname?

A. The Lobster House

B. The Candy Castle

C. The Tourist Dungeon

D. The Wedding Cake House

(D) The Wedding Cake House. The gothic-style Wedding Cake House at 104 Summer Street in Kennebunk features multiple pinnacles and elaborate woodwork.

Maine's first lottery was established in 1832 by an act of the Maine Legislature to help fund what project?

A. Cumberland and Oxford Canal

B. Portland Lobster Company

C. The Maine Stagecoach Route

D. The First Annual Lumberjack Festival

(A) Cumberland and Oxford Canal. The lottery was authorized to help raise $50,000 for the canal that would connect the largest lakes west of Portland with the seaport. The Canal Bank of Portland was chartered in 1825 to finance the project.

Under the brand name Belle of Maine, S. Wells & Sons in Wilton, Maine is the only cannery in the world to pack this product:

A. Dandelion Greens

B. Crab Grass

C. Spruce Gum

D. Sea Weed

(A) Dandelion greens. S. Wells & Sons is also the only cannery in the U.S. to pack fiddlehead greens and beet greens.

In what year was Portland Head Light automated?

A. 1989

B. 1951

C. 1975

D. 2001

(A) 1989

The 86-foot high Portland Observatory was built on Munjoy Hill in 1807 by Capt. Lemuel Moody. It used flags to signal what information?

A. Approaching Storms

B. The start of Church services

C. Arriving Trains

D. Arriving vessels

(D) Arriving Vessels.

Which poem was not written by Henry Wadsworth Longfellow?

A. "Paul Revere's Ride"

B. "Evangeline: A Tale of Acadie"

C. "The Rainy Days"

D. "The Road Not Taken"

(D) "The Road Not Taken." This famous poem was written by Robert Frost.

"Remember the Maine" is a famous rallying cry. To what is it referring?

A. Battleship *Maine*

B. The Summer of 1969

C. A state line dispute with Massachusetts

D. An advertising slogan to promote Maine lobster.

(A) The battleship *Maine*. On February 15, 1898, the *Maine* was blown up in Havana Harbor after being sent to make diplomatic contact with Cuba. The United States declared war against Spain a few months later, on April 25.

Peak's Island, which is located off Portland, is home to a special museum that was named in the Guinness Book for World Records for having 730 versions of this item:

A. Lobster traps

B. Umbrella covers

C. Cell phone cases

D. Tent covers

(B) Umbrella covers. Nancy Hoffman started the museum in 1996 with a collection of six different cloth covers.

What was the original park name of Acadia National Park?

A. Eden Garden

B. Rockefeller Gardens

C. Thoreau Woods

D. Lafayette National Park

(D) Lafayette National Park. The park became a public land preserve in 1916 as Sieur de Monts National Monument and was then elevated to national park status in 1919 as Lafayette. The name was changed to Acadia in 1919.

Casco Bay's most famous sea monster goes by what name?

A. Reny

B. Cassie

C. Smaug

D. Marden

(B) Cassie. According to Earl Brechlin's *Wild! Weird! Wonderful! Maine.*, Cassie the Sea Serpent was first spotted in 1779 in Penobscot Bay by a young sailor named Edward Preble (who later was captain of the USS *Constitution*. Cassie has apparently prowled the waters of Maine from Biddeford to Eastport for decades and decades. Cassie, estimated to be between 60 and 125 feet long, was spotted near Portland in 1818 and off Mount Desert Rock in 1836. The most detailed sighting was reported by two fishermen in Casco Bay in 1958.

A fanciful sea monster detail from an early map of the Gulf of Maine. Image courtesy of Library of Congress.

May Davidson, author of the memoir, *Whatever it Takes*, and her husband Jim worked at a variety of jobs including chicken farming, truck driving, and lobster fishing, until they found success by inventing this iconic Maine gift product in the 1980s.

A. The Maine Buoy Bell

B. Moose Poop jewelry

C. Puffin Back Scratcher

D. Lobster Ashtray

(A) The Maine Buoy Bell

What does the Maine word "Daow"(dow) mean?

A. No

B. Part of a boat

C. A dark color

D. An ugly cow

(A) No. Actually, an emphatic "No."

"Didja pay a lot for that new truck?"

"Daow! I got a helluva deal!"

The infamous area between Bangor's Front and Broad Streets was a notorious place in the mid-1800s where loggers and sailors gathered to spend their money on illegal alcohol and prostitutes. What was its name?

A. Hell's Half Acre

B. Devil's Half Acre

C. Purgatory on the Penobscot

D. Lumberjack Lane

(B) Devil's Half Acre

Before the Portland Sea Dogs, this minor league baseball team played in Portland in 1949:

A. Portland Fish

B. Portland Pilots

C. Portland Tourists

D. Portland Sailors

(B) Portland Pilots

What iconic product did Union native Dr. Augustin Thompson create and market as "Nerve Food"?

A. Moxie

B. Whoopie Pies

C. Red Hot Dogs

D. Bubble Gum

(A) Moxie. Thompson changed the tonic first known as "impregnated water" to the beverage called "Moxie Nerve Food." From 1900 to the 1920s, Moxie was America's most popular soft drink. Not surprisingly, it was President Calvin (Silent Cal) Coolidge's favorite beverage. Today, there is still an annual Moxie Festival in Lisbon Falls that takes place every July to celebrate the famous drink.

Every October, the Sunday River Ski Resort in Newry hosts this championship competition.

A. North American Wife-Carrying Championship

B. Egg Toss Championship

C. Coffee Brandy Drinking Championship

D. Log-Rolling Championship

(A) North American Wife-Carrying Championship. Male contestants must traverse a 278-yard obstacle course while carrying a woman. In 2021, the winners received the woman's weight in beer, five times her weight in cash, and an entry into the World Championship, which took place in Finland the following summer.

This business, known locally as Maine Yankee, was commissioned in 1972 after four years of construction that cost more than $231 million dollars. It closed in 1996.

A. Paper Mill

B. Sardine Factory

C. Railroad

D. Nuclear Power Plant

(D) Nuclear Power Plant

In 1820, the year Maine became a state, its total population was:

A. 75,896

B. 298,335

C. 505,420

D. 762,119

(B) 298,335

This 31-foot tall statue was a gift from a group of New York builders. It is now an iconic piece of art in Bangor. Who or what does it depict or honor?

A. A Black Bear

B. A Sailor

C. USS *Maine*

D. Paul Bunyan

(D) Paul Bunyan. Paul Bunyan is a mythical lumberjack in American and Canadian folklore.

During the 2018 Skowhegan Fair, more than 1,000 people gathered at grandstands to set a Guinness Record for what?

A. The World's Largest Pancake

B. The World's Largest Line Dance

C. The World's Biggest Moose Call

D. The World's Largest Demolition Derby

(C) The World's Biggest Moose Call. The record for moose calling was set on June 9, 2018. There is no record if any moose responded.

What important item—essential to all year-round Mainers—was invented by Don Sargent of Bangor?

A. Coffee brandy

B. Earmuffs

C. The snowplow

D. The woodstove

(C) The snowplow.

The Portland Sea Dogs are a minor league baseball team based in Portland. Prior to the Sea Dogs, which of these minor league baseball teams also called Portland home?

A. Portland Gulls

B. Portland Eskimos

C. Portland Duffs

D. All of the above.

(D) All of the above. Other teams included the Portland Phenoms and the Portland Parmounts.

In the late 1800s, the Electrolytic Marine Salts Company opened in Lubec. It raised money and sold shares by claiming it had invented a process to extract what from sea water?

A. Silver

B. Gold

C. Mermaids

D. Diamonds

(B) Gold. In the late 1800s, two Massachusetts men claimed to have developed a method of extracting gold from seawater. In 1897, the two men, Reverend Prescott Jernegan and Charles Fisher, bought an old gristmill in Lubec which they converted into the Electrolytic Marine Salts Company. The two men claimed that millions of dollars (as much as $100 million) were flowing through the Lubec Narrows every day, and that by using special "accumulators," which they had invented, gold could be extracted from seawater. Hundreds of thousands of shares in the company were sold for one dollar each, dozens of workers were hired, and operations began. The first factory was going so well, they made plans to build a second factory and employ hundreds of people. However, in 1898, the two men mysteriously vanished from town, leaving bewildered townspeople and defrauded investors behind. According to some reports, Reverend Jernegan traveled to France under an assumed name and later returned a small portion of the money to his investors.

Extra Credit

True or False: In the 1830s, the State of Maine sent 10,000 troops into the Aroostook Valley region in anticipation of war with our neighbors in Canada?

True.

The Aroostook War was an undeclared and bloodless war that flared up because England and the United States could not agree on the borderline between our country and the Canadian province of New Brunswick. Since way, way back, the Brits had claimed all the land above Mars Hill. I can already hear the cynical "Northern Massachusetts" readers among you saying, "Wait, the good people of America were prepared to fight and die for whatever exists above Mars Hill?"

In a word, yes. By this time, we had more than just about had it with the British, so in January of 1839, a land agent named Rufus McIntire took a posse into the disputed area and started arresting innocent Canadian lumberjacks who were cutting down trees on disputed land. It was not really a surprise when Rufus was eventually arrested by Canadian officials. At this point, Mainers were wicked annoyed and decided they really, really wanted all the land above Mars Hill. So, within two months there were about 10,000 Maine troops either encamped along the Aroostook River or marching toward the hot spot.

Down in Washington, the federal government authorized a force of 50,000 men and a budget of $10 million in the event a hot war broke out. At this point, the Brits—convinced that they'd stirred up a hornet's nest—decided to talk peace, and after a few sessions of haggling and dickering, they eventually signed the Webster-Ashburton Treaty in 1842, which set the line between Canada and Maine once and for all.

Finish this famous advertising slogan: "I should have bought it when I . . ."?

". . . saw it at Marden's."

Harold "Micky" Marden built a Maine retailing icon after opening his first store in Fairfield in 1964. The family-owned chain has fourteen stores from Madawaska to Calais to Sanford. Marden's is famous for locating and purchasing overstocks, closeouts, insurance losses, liquidations, salvage deals, discontinued items, and other deals across the country and selling them at discounted prices.

Where did the term "crow flies" originate?

The term "crow flies," is an idiom for the most direct path between two points and may have nautical roots. According to one legend, back in the age of sail (long before GPS and radar systems), mariners brought caged crows on board their vessel. When sailors didn't know where the nearest land was, they would release a crow. Because crows are not water birds, they would fly straight toward the nearest land. The crow cages were kept high on the mast in what became known as the crow's nest. There are some who would dispute that origin, but it is generally accepted that the first written use of the term "straight as the crow flies" was by Charles Dickens in his 1838 novel *Oliver Twist*.

Why is Maine located "Down East?"

Buckle up buttercup, this is going to take some 'splaining. Even now in the twenty-first century there's a lot that's still murky about the ubiquitous word, or words, "Downeast" or "Down East" as some would have it. We still can't agree on whether it's a single word or a two-word phrase. And that's just the beginning of the problem.

A question you often get from summer complaints is: "How come they call a place that looks like it is really 'up north'— Down East?" It's a good question, and I'm sure there are all kinds of clever, sarcastic answers we could come up with here, but for the time being we'll try to avoid the temptation. To get the actual answer you have to go back to the nineteenth century when most everything in and out of Maine arrived and departed on sailing vessels.

The easiest trip for sailors to take out of Boston was to Maine, since prevailing winds along the New England coast often blew from southwest to northeast. If you were on a schooner sailing from Boston to Maine you could expect a pleasant down-wind sail to the northeast. To continue this, you could say that the least popular voyage for nineteenth-century sailors was an up-wind sail from Maine to Boston.

When a sailor in Boston was asked where he was off to he might say he was heading to Maine. But rather than drag the whole thing out and say "I'm taking a down-wind sail to the Northeast," he would simply say I'm heading Down East.

In the sixties some old timers in Maine would insist that if you were going to a ball game at Fenway Park you were going "up" to Boston and when the game was over you'd leave Boston and come back "down" to Maine.

So, it all goes back to the days when schooners ruled the waves in these parts and many of the phrases of sailors became the phrases of Maine. At least that's our story and we are sticking to it.

Where does Down East begin?

Trick question. No one really knows.

Sailors in the old days considered it to be any destination from Maine to the Maritime Provinces of Canada. I once asked a new arrival to Portland if they'd ever been Down East and he matter-of-factly stated: "I've been to Freeport." Now, most everyone would admit that Freeport has more claim to the designation Down East than Fryberg but just barely.

Most people in Portland and further south agree that you're not really Down East until you get up to about Bath, the shipbuilding town on the Kennebec River. In Bath you might be told that you have to go beyond Thomaston to Rockland if you want to get the feel for Down East.

In Rockland they're likely to laugh right in your face and then tell you to keep on truckin' because you won't even get a good whiff of Down East until you get to the former broiler capital of the world—Belfast.

By now you should begin to catch on so you won't even stop in Belfast you'll just keep going. In Searsport you might stop and someone there will tell you that you're getting closer, but that you'll have to get east of Ellsworth before you're in the vicinity of Down East.

This will go on and on until you finally find yourself in the visitor parking lot at West Quoddy Head Light, the easternmost point of land in the United States. Then you'll scratch your head and wonder—as many have wondered before you—why is the easternmost point of land Down East called WEST Quoddy Head?

What should you do if you meet a black bear in the Maine woods?

Back away slowly; do not turn and run.

That reminds us of a bear story. A couple of years ago, this fella from New Jersey came to Maine to see what it was like to spend a week in the Great North Woods.

This fella hired himself a Maine guide from down to Grand Lake Stream by answering an ad in a sportsman's magazine. And he got one of the best, Murray Seavey. Murray picked this fella up at the Bangor International Airport, loaded his fancy, new gear into the truck, and headed to his camp up-country.

As they drove along, the New Jersey fella looked out the window at the miles and miles of woods and began to wonder just what it was he was getting himself into. Being born and raised in the city, he'd never spent much time around trees—at least, not as many as he now saw through the truck window as they sped down the road.

For years he had talked about having what people in the city call "a wilderness experience," or what Mainers call "a trip to camp." And now, here he was.

When they got to camp Murray got right to work setting things up. By now the New Jersey fella was so nervous about being in the wild woods of Maine that he was afraid to let Murray out of his sight, and followed him around camp like a puppy.

At one point Murray finally turned to him and said, "Look, why don't you make yourself useful and take that bucket down to the spring and get us some water while I finish building us a fire in the stove for supper."

Wanting to be agreeable, the fella took the bucket and went out the door, down the path to the spring. Five minutes later he was back, white as a ghost, the bucket in his hand rattling away.

Murray took one look at him and said, "What in the world is wrong with you?"

The fella from New Jersey said, "Well, I went down to the spring like you asked me, and when I got there I saw what must have been a three-hundred-pound black bear standing right up to his waist in the spring!"

"And that's what's got you all scared to death?" Murray asked, scratching his beard.

"Well, yes," said the New Jersey fella, a little annoyed at Murray's reaction.

"Let me tell you something," said Murray. "I guarantee you, that black bear was as scared of you as you were of him!"

"Is that true?" asked the fella, now a tad embarrassed.

"That is absolutely true," said Murray, emphatically.

"In that case," said the fella, with a little chuckle, "that spring water isn't fit to drink, now, anyway."

In what Month was the "traditional" town meeting held?

March.

If the traditional New England town meeting didn't exist, we here in Maine would have to invent it just to add a tad of excitement to our lives at this thrill-challenged time of year. They say when our colonial ancestors first started experimenting with the town meeting concept they tried scheduling their meetings in other months, but after a long period of trial and error New England towns finally settled on March because, as they rightly observed, March is unquestionably the most useless stretch of days ever to occur on a calendar made by humans.

Think about it. What else is there for decent hard-working citizens in Maine to do in the dreary month of March but sit around a heat-challenged town hall for three or four hours and argue with neighbors about the condition of the town's roads and how much should be spent to make them passable? Even those rare towns among us that are inhabited only by enlightened citizens and therefore usually have no known problems can easily conjure up one or two in March, when the rotten weather has a way of making even the most ideal situations worse than what they really are.

Those who are into conspiracies—and who isn't these days?—like to think that town meetings were set in March by ruthless town road commissioners. They argue that no one in their right mind would vote against a road budget, however bloated, after riding over a few miles of the town's disintegrating roads. The ride to town meeting in March is an argument to spend whatever it'll take to get the roads back in shape.

It's also said that anyone in Maine still in their right mind makes plans to be enjoying the sunny climes of our country's southern regions about the time March arrives in Maine. So just who's voting at these town meetings, anyway?

Some of Maine's trendy towns—with no respect for stodgy New England tradition—have abandoned March meetings altogether and now have their town meetings in unsuitable months like July, or worse yet, August. But, in March, we're much less likely to be busy with pesky out-of-state visitors and more likely to attend. Also, you can't work in the woods in March because of mud season, and for the same reason you couldn't do much plowing or planting in your fields, either. What better time to get together and get all the town's unpleasant business out of the way before the nice weather arrives?

Maine is bordered by only one other state. How many other continental states share only one border?

None.

Maine is the only state that is bordered by only one other state. Unfortunately for us, the one state we border is New Hampshire. Just kidding!

All seriousness aside, we love our "Live Free or Die!" neighbors. However, there is always some bickering about exactly where the border lies. I remember a few years ago, I heard a team of surveyors was hired by Maine and New Hampshire to try to set the border once and for all.

One day they were working in Oxford County, and after spending a day going through swamps and fields and pucker-brush, they realized that a farm on the border was not in Maine at all, but was actually in New Hampshire.

One of the surveyors was given the task of telling the owner the news. The surveyor fella was a little concerned because he didn't know how the farm's owner would take to being told his farm had just moved from one state to another. He walked up to the farmhouse, called "hello" a few times, and finally, an elderly gentleman came to the door.

"Sir," he said, "I'm with the survey team, straightening out the border here, and after surveying through your farm, we discovered that your place isn't in Maine at all—it's actually in New Hampshire."

The old man looked a little stunned at first, but then said, "Well, thank you, young fella, for that news, and thank the good Lord, too. You know, I was just sitting here wondering how I was going to make it through another Maine winter."

How did Portland's Million Dollar Bridge get its name?

The story goes that when they started building the bridge across the Fore River, between Portland and South Portland, back in 1915, the cost of the bridge kept climbing and climbing until people started saying, "We've got ourselves a million-dollar bridge right there, whether we wanted one or not." That's the story we came up with after "researching" the question. If you've got a better story we'd love to hear it. The bridge was demolished in 1997–1998.

Should you pay the asking price making a purchase at a yard sale in Maine?

NO! Good Heavens, no.

In late spring, yard sale season begins with sale items blooming like dandelions on lawns across Maine.

As this robust state industry awakens to another exciting season of wild, sometimes raucous, completely unregulated and untaxed retail activity—a Libertarian's dream—I thought it would be a good idea to review some of its unique customs, just so you won't be embarrassed by committing a yard sale faux pas. Note that I said "customs." There are no rules for yard sales— that would smack of regulation—but you should know that in yard sale society, "customs" are to be strictly observed.

As you begin your first yard sale tour of the season, there are some things you should keep in mind. First, whenever possible, you should always make your yard sale experience part of a tour. A visit to several sales gives you more variety—and variety is the spice of life. Oh, that reminds me of something else: Never buy spices at a yard sale. I can't remember exactly why you shouldn't, but, as I recall it, there are good reasons.

According to custom, yard sales are made up of items that come very close to being thrown on the town dump or trans-ferred to one of our many modern transfer stations. That's because before any yard sale a family will go through the stacks of stuff they want to get rid of and make two piles, one for the dump, another item for the yard sale. Often, it's a close call. Comments such as, "Oh, throw it on the yard sale pile for now; we can always take it to the dump later," are common during yard sale preparation. The point is, most of the stuff in the average yard sale is pretty close to being worthless. So, anything a family can get from a yard sale is considered "found money."

Another thing to know about yard sales is that when the signs say 8 a.m. to 4 p.m. you shouldn't come pounding on the door at quarter to six in the morning. Early birds are assumed to be dealers and they're difficult enough to deal with at any hour of the day but most difficult before 6 a.m.

Almost as bad are members of the eBay crowd, who like to scour a yard sale or two before breakfast and post a few dozen items online before lunch. Then, while you're slaving away in your yard, the eBayers are sitting with their laptops in the wireless coffee shop down the street keeping track of the bidding on their precious items.

But back to yard sales and the people who visit them.

When you see a worthless item priced at ten dollars sitting before you on a lawn, you should never just whip out a ten and hand it to the yard sale host and move on. In yard sale circles it is considered a violation of yard sale etiquette to pay the asking price for any item, without first giving your host an opportunity to hone his or her haggling skills.

And one more thing. Although yard sales are serious business here in Maine you should try and have fun at the sales you visit, and please don't text us bragging about how much you made selling your yard sale finds on eBay.

Acknowledgments

There have been many, many wonderful books written about the great state of Maine in general and even more dealing with specific aspects of Maine history. And in 2022, there are also many wonderful websites that also offer great information. We used many of these sources to research this book.

The books we reviewed included: *Maine; a Bicentennial History* by Charles E. Clark; *Maine Almanac* by Jim Brunelle; *Maine; a literary chronicle* by W. Storrs Lee; *Maine Trivia* by John N. Cole; *Enjoying Maine* by Bill Caldwell; *Rivers of Fortune* by Bill Caldwell; *Maine My First Pocket Guide* by Carole Marsh; *Yankee Talk* by Robert Hendrickson; *It Happened in Maine* by Gail Underwood Parker; *The Maine Reader: The Down East Experience from 1614 to the Present*, edited by Charles and Samuella Shain; *A Distant War Comes Home: Maine in the Civil War Era*, edited by Donald W. Beattie, Rodney M. Cole, and Charles G. Waugh; *Maine: A Narrative History* by Neil Rolde; *The Story of Bangor: A Brief History of Maine's Queen City*, published by BookMarc's Publishing; *Maine: The Pine Tree State from Prehistory to the Present*, edited by Richard W. Judd, Edwin A. Churchill, and Joel W. Eastman; *Maine: Downeast and Different* by Neil Rolde; *Downeast Genius* by Earl Smith; *Wild! Weird! Wonderful! Maine.* by Earl Brechlin; *Hauling by Hand* by Dean L. Lunt; *Here for Generations* by Dean L. Lunt; and *This Day in Maine* by Joseph Owen. In addition, we visited various websites including the websites developed by the state of Maine and many Maine towns. We also used entries that appear as part of Wikipedia. It was fun to review so many sources and we thank everyone for all the hard work!

About the Authors

Dean Lunt

Dean Lunt was born in the Maine island fishing village of Frenchboro. He attended the island's one-room school and Mount Desert Island High School before earning a dual degree from Syracuse University. Following graduation, he worked as an award-winning newspaper reporter in three New England states for nearly twelve years, and later as a freelance writer, editor, and project manager. Lunt founded Islandport Press in 1999 and has since edited or published more than two hundred books, most tied in some way to the culture and heritage of Maine or New England. Lunt has written five books, including *Hauling by Hand*, *Here for Generations*, and *Voices off the Ocean*. He has two daughters and now lives in Yarmouth with his wife, Michelle.

John McDonald

John McDonald (1944-2022), who was regarded as a dean of Maine storytelling, got his start as a performer playing at local Downeast Maine events in the 1970s before catching his first big break when he was asked to perform on stage with the legendary Marshall Dodge and Kendall Morse at Ellsworth's Strand Theater in 1980. Over the years, McDonald performed for audiences across New England, released two audio recordings, and wrote five books, including the now-classics *A Moose and a Lobster Walk into Bar* and *Down the Road a Piece*. He was also a long-time radio talk show host in Portland.